Clear
and
Present
Thinking

PROJECT DIRECTOR:
Brendan Myers (CEGEP Heritage College)

AUTHORS:
Brendan Myers
Charlene Elsby (Queen's University)
Kimberly Baltzer-Jaray (University of Waterloo)
Nola Semczyszyn (Franklin & Marshall College)

EDITOR / PROOFREADER:
Natalie Evans (University of Guelph - Humber)

LAYOUT AND DESIGN:
Nathaniel Winter-Hébert, Lana Winter-Hébert
www. winterhebert.com

Version 1.1 (21st May 2013)

NORTHWEST PASSAGE BOOKS

ISBN:
978-0-9920059-0-0

For all other enquiries, please visit *brendanmyers.net*

NORTHWEST
PASSAGE
Books

Clear
and
Present
Thinking

A handbook in logic and rationality.

Version 1.1

Northwest Passage Books

Contents

Contents

Acknowledgments

This project was financially supported by the donations of over 700 people, through the Kickstarter.com fundraising platform, including:

Linda Demissy, Jeffrey Wyndham, Jonathan Tapia, Carl Witty, Charlene Elsby, Jennifer Bezanson, Rod MacPherson, Jennifer Hunt, Kadri Weiler, T. Scarlet Jory, Jennifer Hunt, Theo Geer, Teo Bishop, Julien St-Laurent, Tammy Longe, Holly Bird, Nic Daines, Gillian Watson, Chris Rybisky, Sydney Lancaster, Fernando Villasenor, Ruth Merriam, David Burch, Katt Taylor, Kevin L. Krakauer, Matan Nassau, Jon Nebenfuhr, Bill Hovingh, Thomas Darlington, Robin Powell, Peter Wolanski, Fabiola Martin, Cequinne Reyamoir Sky, Robert Moore, Brian Baskerville, Claire Verney, Melissa Kean, Melissa Reid, Ian McNab, Deirdre Hebert, Rory Bowman, Jennifer Neal, Phil Kessler, Nick Warner, Hugh Long, Turlough Myers, Pat Bellavance, Chris Nichols, Michael Brown, Sarah Clements, Stevie Miller, Marcos Gomez, Lisa Tamres, Karen Schreiber, Idalia Nelson, Debbie Carman, T Thorn Coyle, John Beckett, Selene Vega, Soli Johnson, Lianne Lavoie, Jennifer Ramon, Brian Figgins, Amanda Strong, Lydia Ondrusek, Neil Negandhi, Seto Konowa, Bart Salisbury, John Rahael, Nancy Allin, H Lynnea Johnson, Katherine Lawrence, Samuel Basa, Jim Burrows, Robert E. Stutts, Daryn Tsuji, Deanna Victoria, Frederick Polgardy, Elodie Crespel, Walter Erskine, Wilma Jandoc, Nanci Quinn, Rachel Porteous, Teree McCormick, Bailey Shoemaker Richards, Ana de Montvert, Brian Andrew, Nick Mailer, Gavin Lambert, Mike Little, Antonina York, Laura Packer, Cynthia Gresham, Carol Waller, John Pritchard, Mark Cumisky, Ed Kowalczewski, Tamarra Wallace, Cheri Lovell, JD Ferries-Rowe, Maria Laine, Ralph Warnick, Cletus Stell, Lucas York, Jeff Chen, Michael Sena, Lisa Isaacson, Dag Hovden, William Andrews, Bill Dourte, Joseph de Leon, Douglas Bass, Dean Holbrough, Grant Haavaldsrud, Jussi Myllyluoma, Peter C. March, Deborah Spiesz, Evan Grummell, Robert Carnochan, Angela Gallant, Kevin J. Maroney, Stephanie McMillen-Sherry, Md. Muazzam B. Sham Khiruddin, David Lim, Mark Wendelborn, Thomas Bourke, James Husum, Doug Eves, Bruce Becker, Bob Levin, Simon Lieutaud, Steven Hosford, Brian LaShomb, Colin Boswell, John Fox, Jason Piterak, Dirk Renckens, Sam Sabra, Bobby G Berney, Hannah Hiles, Albion Gould, Enrico Chir, Richard L Skubic, Corwin Samuelson, Zac Trolley, Melanie Meixner, Andrew Bowser, Danny Witting, Melinda Reidinger, Graeme Barber, Matthew Slatkin, Barbara Jacobi, Jennifer Mott, Melody Lake, Philipp Schneider, Nicholas Pietrzak, Elizabeth A. Stout, Andrew Ma, Bernadette Martinez, Dominic Caplan, John Baksa, Todd Penland, Christian R. Meloche, Ivan Yagolnikov, John Merklinghaus, Matthew Habermehl, Burrell Crittendon, Scott Morris, Sean Herron, Glenn Slotte, Björn Fonseca, Jay Welshofer, David Fugate, Ty Sawyer, David Sosulski, Damion Moser, Thomas Brincefield, Paul Schultz, Kevin Tibbs, Nicholas Dunne, Chris Felstead, Jim Hill, Jayson Mackie, Matthew Suber, Sam Sgro, Mike Kallies, Garry Crossland, Michael Gradin, John Bernardo, Elena Martinez, Justin Minnes, Ranti Junus, Mark Phelps, Susanne Huttner, Andrea Hess, Simon Ward, Thomas Langenbach,

Acknowledgments

Alex Gibson, Philippe Chanelet, Skye Nathaniel Schiefer, Julian Greene, Jennifer Gibson, James Foster, Kennita Watson, Robert Meeks, Corina Thornton, Hilary Sadowsky, Eric Hortop, Joann Keesey, Alison Lilly, Millard Arnold IV, Adam Daw, Garth Elliott, Mary Henderson, Mike Mallory, JD Hickey, Andrew Dulson, Stanley Yamane, Aurora Jade Pichette, Jennifer M Shaw, Kami Landy, Gaston Croteau, Seonaid Lee, Dan Pierson, Adrienne Dandy, Ealasaid haas, Roland Conybeare, William Blumberg, Regina P. Wade, Christye Gruen, Maria Bement, Michelle Bar-Evan, Raja Thiagarajan, Nicholas George, Larry Wood, Kerry Michalski-Russell, Michael Green, Paul Fischer, Kiran Reddy, Thomas King, Edward Hinkey, Bryce Bederka, Martin Gray, Nick Allott, Jonas Schiött, Sara Korn, Jessica Heaston, Dan Reshef, Kevin Chin, Donald & Sabrina Sutherland, Derric Pruitt, Ben Rossi, Chris Rose, Deanna Jones, David Churn, Solomon Matthews, Judith Wouk, Gary Gibson, Rob C. Agnew, Robert Young, Kay M Purcell, John Benner Jr, Mark Bisignano, Stephen Antonello, Ed Deeley, Jochen Schmiedbauer, Andrew Kwon, John Moreau, James E. Donnelly, Vanessa Smallbon, Niels Nellissen, Elaine Chen Jing, Russell Keenan, Nunzio Bizness, Rochelle McCune, Michelle MacAlpine, Rob Harshman, Kevin McKenzie, David Monreal i Prat, Taylor Judd, Charles Petras, Chrissandra Porter, Katherine Terban, Leon Higley, Yves Lacombe, Martin Kleen, Nathan Malik, Geoff Coxhead, Joe & Alisa Roy, S R Van Keuren, Alex Basson, Carey Head, Carol Bean, Margaret Colville, Valerie Voigt, Leon Samadi, Bruce Spurr, Steven Moy, Elemental Book & Curiosity Shop Inc., David Govoni, Jacob Thias, C.D. Carson, Sheena MacIsaac, Andy Lawton, Rebecca Turner, Ivan Lewis, Ryoji Nakase, Deborah Goldsmith, Truls Bjørvik, James R. Hall, William Healy, Gareth Thomas, Todd Showalter, Russ Neff, Brittany Wilbert, Tobias Ammann, Mj Patterson, Joe Salek, Mostafa Faghfoury, Caroline Kenner, Joshua Smith, Homam Alattar, Mara Georges, Bryan Bonifacio, Chad Hobson, Ryoichi Kinoshita, David O'Brien, Glenn McCrimmon, Susan Grant-Suttie, Mike Smith, Benjamin Wade.

sound   colour

EAR   EYE

THINKING ideas

sm— NOSE —ell

TONGUE

touch SKIN taste

"Thinking … is no more and no less an organ of perception than the eye or ear. Just as the eye perceives colours and the ear sounds, so thinking perceives ideas." – Rudolph Steiner.

What is thinking? It may seem strange to begin a logic textbook with this question. 'Thinking' is perhaps the most intimate and personal thing that people do. Yet the more you 'think' about thinking, the more mysterious it can appear. It is the sort of thing that one intuitively or naturally understands, and yet cannot describe to others without great difficulty. Many people believe that logic is very abstract, dispassionate, complicated, and even cold. But in fact the study of **logic** is nothing more intimidating or obscure than this: **the study of good thinking.**

Before asking what good thinking is, we might want to ask a few questions about thinking as *such*. Let's say that thinking is the activity of the mind. It includes activities like reasoning, perceiving, explaining, inventing, problem solving, learning, teaching, contemplating, knowing, and even dreaming. We think about everything, all the time. We think about ordinary practical matters like what to have for dinner tonight, all the way to the most abstract and serious matters, like the meaning of life. You are thinking, right now, as you read this sentence.

Some may wish to draw a distinction between thinking and feeling, including sense perception, emotional experience, or even religious faith. Some might want to argue that computers or animals are capable of thinking, even if their way of thinking is somehow different from that of humans. And some might say that the question is an absurd one: everyone knows what thinking is, because everyone 'thinks' all the time, and everyone can 'feel' themselves thinking. We are somehow 'aware' of thoughts in our minds, aware of

information and knowledge, aware of memories, and aware of likely future probabilities and so on. Thinking is a first-order phenomenological insight: it's a bit like knowing what the colour 'red' looks like, or knowing the taste of an orange. You know what it is, but you probably have an awfully hard time describing or defining it.

Thinking, in this way of 'thinking' about thinking, is an *event*. It is something *done*, something that *takes place*, and something that *happens*.

There are a lot of serious philosophical (as well as scientific) questions about the nature of thinking. For instance, we might ask: *'who is it that knows that he or she knows?'* Who is it that is aware of thinking? And is not that awareness of thinking itself a kind of thinking? This is a line of questioning that may seem as if it can go on forever. It's a little bit beyond the purpose of this book to investigate all of them. But if you happen to find yourself asking how do you know that you know something, or if you find yourself thinking about the nature of thinking itself, you may be well on your way toward becoming an excellent philosopher!

Why is good thinking important?

A lot of people think of philosophy as something rather vague, wishy-washy, or simplistic. You'll hear people quote a line from a popular song or movie, and then they'll say, "That's my philosophy." But there's a lot more to it than that; and a person who merely repeats a popular saying and calls it philosophy has not been doing enough work. Philosophical questions are often very *difficult* questions, and they demand a lot of effort and consideration and time.

Good and bad thinking are very different from each other. Yet some people might feel personally threatened by this distinction. Your thoughts are probably the most intimate and the most precious of all your possessions. Your mind, indeed, is the only part of you that is truly 'yours', and cannot be taken away from you. Thus if someone tells you that your thinking is muddled, confused, unclear, or just plain mistaken, then you might feel very hurt or very offended.

08

But your thinking certainly *can* be muddled or confused. Normally, bad quality thinking happens when your mind has been 'possessed', so to speak, by other people and made to serve their purposes instead of your own. This can happen in various ways.

In your life so far, you have gathered a lot of beliefs about a lot of different topics. You believe things about who you are, what the world is like, where you belong in the world, and what to do with your life. You have beliefs about what is good music and bad music, what kind of movies are funny and what kind are boring, whether it's right or wrong to get a tattoo, whether the police can be trusted, whether or not there is a god, and so on. These beliefs came from somewhere. Most of you probably gathered your most important beliefs during your childhood. You learned them from your family, especially your parents, your teachers at school, your piano instructor or your karate instructor, your scout group or guide group leader, your priest, your medical doctor, your friends, and just about anybody who had any kind of influence on your life. There is nothing wrong with learning things from other people this way; indeed, we probably couldn't get much of a start in life without this kind of influence. **But if you have accepted your beliefs from these sources, and not done your own thinking about them, then they are not your beliefs, and you are not truly thinking your own thoughts.** They are, instead, someone else's thoughts and beliefs, occupying your mind. If you believe something only because someone else taught it to you, and not because you examined those beliefs on your own, then in an important sense, you are not having your own thoughts. And if you are not having

your own thoughts, then you are not living your own life, and you are not truly free.

Some people might resist studying logic for other reasons. They may prefer to trust their intuition or their "gut feelings" as a source of knowledge. I'm always very curious about such people. Perhaps they think that logic is dispassionate and unemotional, and that logical people end up cold-hearted and emotionless, like robots. Perhaps they find their intuitive beliefs so gratifying that they cannot allow anything to interfere with them. Perhaps they worry that they may have to re-evaluate their beliefs and their lives, and perhaps change their lives as a result of that re-evaluation. Those things may be true for some people, if not for all of them. But when your beliefs are grounded in reason, the quality of your inner life will be far, far better, in ways like these:

- You will be in greater conscious control of your own mind and thoughts.
- It will be harder for advertising, political propaganda, peer pressure, scams and confidence tricks, or other forms of psychological manipulation to affect you.
- When your actions or motives are questioned, you will be much better able to explain yourself effectively and persuasively.
- You will be able to understand difficult, complex, and challenging ideas a lot easier, and with a lot less anxiety.
- You will be able to understand things in a more comprehensive and complete way.
- You will be better able to identify the source of your problems, whether practical or personal, and better able to handle or solve those problems.
- You will feel much less frustrated or upset when you come across something that you do not understand.
- You will be better able to plan for the future, compete for better paying or more prestigious jobs, and to gather political power.
- You will find it easier to stand up to governments, employers, and other authorities when they act unjustly.
- Tragedies, bad fortune, stress, and other problems in life will be easier to deal with.
- You will find it easier to understand other people's feelings and other people's points of view, and you will

be better able to help prevent those differences from becoming conflicts.

- You will get much more pleasure and enjoyment from the arts, music, poetry, science, and culture.
- You may even enjoy life more than you otherwise would.

Let me add that the use of reason doesn't shut out one's feelings, or the benefit of the arts or of human relationships, or any of the apparently non-logical things that make life enjoyable and fun. Indeed, in classical and mediaeval philosophy reason was said to be the very presence of God within the human soul. It is by means of reason that a human being could get inside the mind of God, and obtain an experience of eternity. Reason can be a spiritual thing. But, alas, I'll have to discuss that prospect in more detail another time.

There are also social and public benefits to being able to reason well. Over the centuries, thoughtful individuals and their associates used reason, evidence, argument, scientific observation and persuasion to work for a more free, peaceful and just society. Consider a few examples:

WANG ANSHI (11th century): Chinese economist who transformed the civil service examination system to prevent nepotism. He instituted various reforms in government to protect the rights of the poor, especially poor farmers.

MARTIN LUTHER (1483-1546): Christian monk from Saxony, who translated the Bible into vulgate German so that ordinary people could read it and decide for themselves what it meant. His public condemnations of corrupt practices in the Roman Church (especially including the sale of indulgences) led to the creation of Protestantism.

NELLIE McCLUNG (1873-1951): Canadian politician who, together with four associates (the 'Famous Five'), campaigned to change Canadian law so that women would be recognized as persons. This allowed women to vote and to be appointed to the Senate.

EDWARD R. MURROW (1908-1965): American journalist and broadcaster. He was one

of the first reporters to describe to the world the crimes against humanity, which took place at the Buchenwald Nazi concentration camp. He also systematically exposed, and effectively stopped, the Communist conspiracy paranoia promoted by Wisconsin Senator Joseph McCarthy.

WILLIAM WILBERFORCE (1759-1833): British evangelical Christian who was the most influential voice in the movement to abolish slavery in the British empire in 1807.

VACLAV HAVEL (1936-2011): Playwright, poet, and political activist who campaigned against unjust prosecutions. Eventually becoming President of Czechoslovakia, he oversaw the dismantling of communism in his country, and of the Warsaw Pact military alliance.

FLORENCE NIGHTINGALE (1820-1910): Military nurse during the Crimean War, who secularized and expanded the profession of nursing, and who campaigned for the improvement of public health in the British Empire.

JULIAN ASSANGE (born 1971-): Australian journalist and computer programmer who campaigns for press freedom, and who founded WikiLeaks, an international whistleblowing organization which publishes leaked secret documents in order to publicize and prevent the unjust or criminal actions of corporations and governments.

In their own time, many of these people were ridiculed or persecuted. Some of them were, and still are, controversial figures, because of other things they did (or allegedly did). But all of them changed the world for the better, in great or small ways, and at great personal risk, through the courageous use of their intelligence. I'm going to be bold here and claim that **every successful social reformer the world has ever known has also been a rational and critical thinker and speaker**. Regardless of their profession, every successful social and political reform was made possible by people who carefully and logically observed, examined and judged the world around them. Even great religious prophets and their supporters had to show that their teachings could withstand rational

09

scrutiny, and were not simply, nor only, a matter of revelation.

By studying logic and critical thinking, you will be equipping yourself with the same skills that enabled them, and people like them, to become heroes. As an exercise, see if you can think of more people to add to this list, and give a few reasons to support why they belong there.

Is logic difficult?

10 You might hear people say that they are no good at math, or at computer programming, or at some other kind of activity that requires a lot of concentration. When I was in high school, I used to believe that I was very bad at math. I resented going to math classes, and so I didn't study, and (therefore!) scored poorly on tests and exams. But one day I found myself making my own video games on my Commodore 128 computer, with no other help besides the dictionary of commands. Then a few years later I was coding HTML scripts by hand, which I learned to do by reading the source codes of other people's web sites. I eventually realized that I was actually rather good at math, or rather that I could be really good at it if I really wanted to be.

Thinking rationally and critically is much the same thing. It's actually fairly easy, once you get into the habit of doing it. Most people are born with an ability to perform complex computational tasks built right into their brains. It's true that we often make mistakes when we try to calculate big numbers in our heads, or when we try to calculate probabilities without much information to start with. Nonetheless, the ability to think deliberately, precisely, and analytically is a large part of what it is to be human. Indeed, every human language, all 8,000 or so of them, have complex computational operators built right into the grammar and syntax, which we use to speak and be understood about anything we may want to talk about. When we study logic, we study (among other things) those very operators as they work themselves out, not only in our thinking, but also in our speaking to each other, and in many of the ways we relate to each other and the

world. Logic examines not what people ought to think, but it examines how we actually do think – when we are thinking clearly!

Here's a very short exercise which may help to show you that you already have within your mind everything you need to understand logic and critical reasoning. Consider the following two sentences:

1. All men are mortal.
2. Socrates is a man.

As almost anyone can see, these two sentences have a relationship to each other. For one thing, there's a topic of discussion that appears in both of them: 'men'. Both sentences also follow the same grammatical structure: they name an object and they name at least one property that belongs to, or can be attributed to, that object. But they also have another, more subtle relation to each other. That subtle relation tells you what should follow next. Here are three possibilities:

a. Therefore, we're having Greek tonight!
b. Therefore, Socrates is a nerd.
c. Therefore, Socrates is mortal.

To most people, the answer is so obvious that I don't need to state which one it is. That's because logical and rational thinking, as already mentioned, is something we all naturally do, all the time.

That example, it may interest you to know, was used by the philosopher Aristotle more than two thousand years ago, and it is still a favourite among philosophy teachers today: we use it as a way of tipping the hat to our predecessors.

Let's look at two more examples, which might show a little more of how that subtle relation works.

1. All the houses built in that neighbourhood are post-war bungalows.
2. My house is in that neighbourhood.
3. Therefore –
   a. My house is a rotting, decrepit shack.
   b. My house is a grand chateau.
   c. Long John Silver was a rotten businessman.

d. My house is a post-war bungalow.

1. Every morning, if it is going to be a sunny day, the rooster in the yard crows.
2. Tomorrow is probably going to be a sunny day, just like the last few days.
3. Therefore –
    a. That rooster is more reliable as the TV weatherman.
    b. One of these days, I'm going to kill that horrible creature!
    c. My old clock on the wall is a family heirloom.
    d. Tomorrow morning, that rooster will probably crow again.

1. If the surprise birthday present is a Harry Potter book, it will be a great gift.
2. The surprise birthday present is a Harry Potter book.
3. Therefore –
    a. I'm going to hide in my bedroom for a few hours.
    b. I really owe the person who gave it to me a big thank-you!
    c. I have to fix the leaky roof over the kitchen today.
    d. It's a great gift.

In each of these examples, the best answer is option D. So long as the first two statements are true, then the third one, option D, *must* be true. You also know that in both examples, option C doesn't belong. It has nothing to do with the two statements that came before it. To claim that option C should come next is *not logical*. Perhaps option C would make sense if it was part of a joke, or a very complicated discussion of housing development plans for pirates, or inheritance laws involving clocks and farm animals, or how author J.K. Rowling doesn't like leaky houses. But in these examples, we do not have that extra information. Going only with the information that we have been given, option C cannot be the correct answer. The best answer, in each case, is option D. Of all the four options offered here, option D has the strongest support from the statements that came before it.

But look again at the options A and B in all three examples. These options were not as silly as option

C. They *might* follow correctly and logically from the statements that came before them, if only we had a little bit more information. Without your deliberate, conscious awareness, your mind probably filled in that extra information with statements like these ones:

1. Maybe all the postwar bungalows in this neighbourhood are rotting, decrepit shacks.
2. Maybe the rooster has never got it wrong so far, unlike the TV weatherman, who makes mistakes all the time.
3. The reason I'll be hiding in my bedroom is because I will want to read the book without anybody disturbing me.
4. People who give great gifts deserve to be thanked.

None of these statements appeared among the initial premises of the argument. Nothing in the initial premises told you anything about these possibilities. They come from outside the argument as presented so far. But that subtle relation between statements allowed you to add something consistent and plausible to the argument in order to move the argument from the premises you had, to conclusions A or B. You might even fill the space with more than one sentence to make the move, as we did in the third possibility above.

Logic is the study of relations among ideas like these. If you could handle these three examples here with ease, then you can handle *everything else in this textbook* just as easily.

The Process of Reasoning

The chapters of this book roughly follow a path that I shall refer to as 'The Process of Reasoning'. In the first chapter, I will describe the 'backdrop' or the 'setting' in which this process takes place. This backdrop consists of **problems**, **intellectual environments**, and **world views**. The next chapters follow the stages of the 'Process of Reasoning' itself, which are:

OBSERVE AND QUESTION. This first stage requires us to gather as much information as we can about one's situation and one's problems. This stage is studied

11

in chapters 1 and 2, where we discuss questions, and various good and bad thinking habits.

EXAMINE POSSIBILITIES. This stage teaches a few techniques and skills that can help us tell the difference between good and bad answers to your questions. We study these skills in chapters 3 and 4, when we look at arguments and fallacies.

MAKE YOUR DECISION. The process of reasoning almost always ends with some kind of judgment or choice, or decision to be made, whether it's a decision about what to believe or about what to do. This stage is covered in chapters 5 and 6, when we look at reasonable doubt and moral reasoning.

OBSERVE AND QUESTION AGAIN. The last stage involves observing and questioning one's decisions, and the consequences that may have followed from them, which brings us back to the beginning of the process.

This is the Basic edition of "Clear and Present Thinking." An expanded edition is currently in preparation, which will offer guidance for examining answers and making decisions in specific fields such as science, religion, politics, economics, and so on.

Communities

Pop Music   Facebook

Politics   Social Club

Television   School

College   Street

City   Movie

Friends   Bar

Science   Park

Media   Legal

Family   University

Religion   Youtube

Twitter   Market

Home   Sport

Art

Chapter One: Questions, Problems, and World Views

Before getting into any of the more analytic details of logical reasoning, let's consider the ways in which ideas 'play out' in the world, and the way we arrive at most of our beliefs. Most textbooks on modern logic assert that the basic unit of logic is the statement – a simple sentence which can be either true or false. But it seems to me that statements have to come from somewhere, and that they do not emerge from nothing. People do not come to believe things at random, or by magic. To my mind, the most obvious places where statements are born are one's intellectual environments, one's problems, and the questions that you and others in your environment tend to ask. Good thinking also begins in situations which prompt the mind to think differently about what it has taken for granted so far.

1.1 Intellectual Environments

Where does thinking happen? This may sound as if it's a bit of a silly question. Thinking, obviously, happens in your mind. But people do more than just think their own thoughts to themselves. People also share their thoughts with each other. Thoughts do not remain confined within your own brain: they also *express themselves* in your words and your actions. I'd like to go out on a bit of a limb here, and say that thinking happens not only in your mind, but **also any place where two or more people gather to talk to one another and share their ideas with each other**. In short, thinking happens wherever two or more people could have a dialogue with each other. In that dialogue, at least two people (but possibly many more) can express, share,

trade, move around, examine, criticize, affirm, reject, modify, argue about, and generally communicate their own and each other's ideas.

The importance of dialogue in reasoning is perhaps most important, and also most obvious, when we are reasoning about moral matters. The philosopher Charles Taylor said:

> Reasoning in moral matters is always reasoning with somebody. You have an interlocutor, and you start from where that person is, or with the actual difference between you; you don't reason from the ground up, as though you were talking to someone who recognized no moral demands whatever. [1]

What Taylor says about moral reasoning also applies to other things we reason about. Whenever you have a conversation with someone about whether something is right, wrong, true, false, partially both, and so on, you do not start the conversation from nothing. Rather, you start from your own beliefs about such things, and the beliefs held by your partner in the conversation, and the extent to which your beliefs are the same, or different, as those of the other person. It is not by accident that Plato, one of the greatest philosophers in history, wrote his books in the form of dialogues between Socrates and his friends. Similarly, French philosopher Michel Foucault observed that especially among Roman writers, philosophy was undertaken as a social practice, often within institutional structures like schools, but also through informal relations like friendships and families. This

---

1 Taylor, <u>Malaise of Modernity</u>, pg. 32

social aspect of one's thinking was considered normal and even expected:

> When, in the practice of the care of the self, one appealed to another person in whom one recognised an aptitude for guidance and counseling, one was exercising a right. And it was a duty that one was performing when one lavished one's assistance on another...[2]

So, to answer the question 'Where does thinking happen?' we can say: 'any place where two or more people can have a conversation with each other about the things that matter to them'. And there are lots of such places. Where the Romans might have listed the philosophy schools and the political forums among those places, we today could add:

- Movies, television, pop music, and the entertainment industry
- Internet-based social networks like Facebook and YouTube
- Streets, parks, and public squares
- Pubs, bars, and concert venues
- Schools, colleges, and universities
- Mass media
- Religious communities and institutions
- The arts
- The sciences
- Courtrooms and legal offices
- Political settings, whether on a small or large scale
- The marketplace, whether local or global
- Your own home, with your family and friends
- Can you think of any more places like this?

In each of the places where thinking happens, there's a lot of activity. Questions are asked, answers are explored, ideas are described, teachings are presented, opinions are argued over, and so on. Some questions are treated as more relevant than others, and some answers meet with greater approval than others. It often happens that in the course of this huge and complicated exchange, some ideas become more influential and more prevalent than others. You find this in the way certain words, names, phrases or definitions

get used more often. And you find it as certain ways to describe, define, criticize, praise, or judge things are used more often than others. The ideas that are expressed and traded around in these ways and in these places, and especially the more *prevalent* ideas, form **the intellectual environment** that we live in.

Most of the time, your intellectual environment will roughly correspond to a social environment: that is, it will correspond (at least loosely) to a group of people, or a community that you happen to be part of. Think about all the groups and communities that you belong to, or have belonged to at one time or another:

- Families
- Sports teams
- The student body of your college
- The members of any social club you have joined
- The people at your workplace
- Your religious group (if you are religious)
- People who live in the same neighbourhood of your town or city
- People who speak the same language as you
- People who are roughly the same age as you
- People who come from the same cultural or ethnic background
- People who like the same music, movies or books as you
- People who play most of the same games as you
- Can you think of any more?

An intellectual environment will have a character of its own. That is, in one place or among one group of people, one idea or group of related ideas may be more prevalent than other ideas. In another place and among other people, a different set of ideas may dominate things. Furthermore, several groups may have very similar intellectual environments, or very different ones, or overlapping ones. Also note that you probably live in more than one social environment, and so you are probably hearing ideas from more than one intellectual environment too.

An intellectual environment, with its prevalent ideas, surrounds everyone almost all the time, and it profoundly influences the way people think. It's where we learn most of our basic ideas about life and the

2 Foucault, <u>The Care of the Self</u>, pg. 53

world, starting at a very early age. It probably includes a handful of stock words and phrases that people can use to express themselves and be understood right away. This is not to say that people get all of their thoughts from their environment. Obviously, people can still do their own thinking wherever they are. And this is not to say that the contents of your intellectual environment will always be the same from one day to the next. The philosopher Alasdair MacIntyre observed that an intellectual tradition is often a continuity of conflict, and not just a continuity of thought. But this is to say that wherever you are, and whatever community you happen to be living in or moving through, the prevalent ideas that are expressed and shared by the people around you will influence your own thinking and your life in profound and often unexpected ways.

By itself, this fact is not something to be troubled about. Indeed, in your early childhood it was probably very important for you to learn things from the people around you. For instance, it was better for a parent to tell you not to touch a hot barbecue with your bare hand, than for you to put your hand there yourself and find out what it feels like. But as you grow into adulthood, it becomes more and more important to know what one's intellectual environment is really like. It is very important to know what ideas are prevalent there, and to know the extent to which those ideas influence you. For if you know the character and content of the intellectual environment in which you live, you will be much better able to do your own thinking. You might end up agreeing with most, or even all of the prevalent ideas around you. But you will have agreed with them for your own reasons, and not (or not primarily) because they are the ideas of the people around you. And that will make an enormous difference in your life.

Some intellectual environments are actually hostile to reason and rationality. Some people become angry, feel personally attacked, or will deliberately resist the questioning of certain ideas and beliefs. Indeed, some intellectual environments hold that intellectual thinking is bad for you! Critical reasoning sometimes takes great courage, especially when your thoughts go against the prevalent ideas of the time and place where you live.

1.2 World Views

Eventually, the ideas that you gathered from your intellectual environment, along with a few ideas of your own that you developed along the way come together in your mind. They form in your mind a kind of plan, a picture, or a model of what the world is like, and how it acts, and so on. This plan helps you to understand things, and also helps you make decisions. Philosophers sometimes call this plan a **world view**.

Think for a moment about some of the biggest, deepest and most important questions in human life. These questions might include:

- What should I do with my life? Where should I go from here? Should I get married? What career should I pursue? Where is my place in the world? How do I find it? How do I create it?
- Is there a God? What is God like? Is there one god, or many gods? Or no gods at all? And if there is, how do I know? And if there's not, how do I know?
- Why are we here? Why are we born? Is there any point to it all?
- What is my society really like? Is it just or unjust? And what is Justice?
- Who am I? What kind of person do I want to be?
- What does it mean to be an individual? What does it mean to be a member of society?
- What happens to us when we die?
- What do I have to do to pass this course?
- Just what are the biggest, deepest and most important questions anyway?

These are philosophical questions. (Well, all but one of them.) Your usual way of thinking about these questions, and others like them is your world view. Obviously, most people do not think about these questions all of the time. We are normally dealing with more practical, immediate problems. What will I have for dinner tonight? If the traffic is bad, how late might I be? Is it time to buy a new computer? What's the best way to train a cat to use the litter-box?

But every once in a while, a limit situation will appear, and it will prompt us to think about higher and deeper things. And then the way that we think about these higher and deeper things ends up influencing the way that we live, the way we make choices, the ways that we relate to other people, and the way we handle almost all of our problems. The sum of your answers to those higher and deeper questions is called your 'world view'.

The word 'world view' was first coined by German philosopher Albert Schweitzer, in a book called "The Decay and Restoration of Civilization", first published in 1923. Actually, the word that Schweitzer coined here is the German word Weltanshauung. There are several possible ways to translate this word. In the text quoted above, as you can see, it's translated as "theory of the universe". It could also be translated as "theory of things" or "world conception". Most English speakers use the simpler and more elegant sounding phrase "world view". Here's how Schweitzer himself defined it:

> The greatest of the spirit's tasks is to produce a theory of the universe. What is meant by a theory of the universe? It is the content of the thoughts of society and the individuals which compose it about the nature and object of the world in which they live, and the position and the destiny of mankind and of individual men within it. What significance has the society in which I live and I myself in the world? What do we want to do in the world? What do we hope to get from it? What is our duty to it? The answer given by the majority to these fundamental questions about existence decides what the spirit is in which they and their age live. (Schweitzer, The Decay and Restoration of Civilization, pg. 80-1)

Schweitzer's idea here is that a world-view is more than a group of beliefs about the nature of the world. It is also a **bridge between those scientific or metaphysical beliefs, and the ethical beliefs about what people can and should do in the world**. It is the intellectual narrative in terms of which the actions, choices, and purposes of individuals and groups make sense. It therefore has indispensable practical utility: it is the justification for a way of life, for individuals and for whole societies. In this sense, a world view is not just something you 'have'; it is also something

that you 'live with'. And we cannot live without one. "For individuals as for the community," Schweitzer said, "life without a theory of things is a pathological disturbance of the higher capacity for self-direction." (Schweitzer, ibid, pg. 86)

Let's define a world view as follows: **A world view is the sum of a set of related answers to the most important questions in life**. Your own world view, whatever it is, will be the sum of your own answers to your philosophical questions, whatever you take those questions to be, and whether you have thought about them consciously or not. Thus your world view is intimately tied to your sense of who you are, how you want to live, how you see your place in your world and the things that are important to you. Not only your answers to the big questions, but also your choice of which questions you take to be the big questions, will form part of your world view. And by the way, that's a big part of why people don't like hearing criticism. A judgment of a world view is often taken to be a judgment of one's self and identity. But it doesn't have to be that way.

Some world views are so widely accepted by many people, perhaps millions of people, and are so historically influential, perhaps over thousands of years, that they have been given names. Here are a few examples:

MODERNISM: referring to the values associated with contemporary western civilization, including democracy, capitalism, industrial production, scientific reasoning, human rights, individualism, etc.

HELIOCENTRISM: the idea that the sun is at the centre of our solar system, and that all the planets (and hundreds of asteroids, comets, minor planets, etc.) orbit around the sun.

DEMOCRACY: the idea that the legitimacy of the government comes from the will of the people, as expressed in free and fair elections, parliamentary debate, etc.

CHRISTIANITY: The idea that God exists; that humankind incurred an 'original sin' due to the events in the Garden of Eden, and that God became Man in the person of Jesus to redeem humanity of its original sin.

ISLAM: The idea that God exists, and that Mohammed was the last of God's prophets, and that we attain blessedness when we live by the five pillars of submission: daily prayer, charity, fasting during Ramadan, pilgrimage to Mecca, and personal struggle.

MARXISM: The idea that all political and economic corruption stems from the private ownership of the means of production, and that a more fair and just society is one in which working class people collectively own the means of production.

DEEP ECOLOGY: The idea that there is an important metaphysical correlation between the self and the earth, or that the earth forms a kind of expanded or extended self; and that therefore protecting the environment is as much an ethical requirement as is protecting oneself.

THE AGE OF AQUARIUS / THE NEW AGE: The idea that an era of peace, prosperity, spiritual enlightenment, and complete happiness is about to dawn upon humankind. The signs of this coming era of peace can be found in astrology, psychic visions, Tarot cards, spirit communications, and so on.

And some of these world views may have other, sub-views bundled inside them. For instance:

Democracy	a. Liberalism
	b. Conservatism
	c. Democratic Socialism
Buddhism	a. Mahayana
	b. Theravada
	c. Tibetan Bon-Po
	d. Zen

Clearly, not all world views are the same. Some have different beliefs, different assumptions, different explanations for things, and different plans for how people should live. Not only do they produce different answers to these great questions, but they often start out with different great questions. Some are so radically different from each other that the people who subscribe to different world views might find it very difficult to understand each other.

In summary, your world view and the intellectual environment in which you live, when taken together,

form the basic background of your thinking. They are the source of most of our ideas about nearly everything. If you are like most people, your world view and your intellectual environment overlap each other: they both support most of the same ideas. Sometimes there will be slight differences between them; sometimes you may find differences so large that you may feel that one of them must be seriously wrong, in whole or in part. Differing world views and differing intellectual environments often lead to social and personal conflict. It can be very important, therefore, to consciously and deliberately know what your own world view really is, and to know how to peacefully sort out the problems that may arise when you encounter people who have different world views.

1.3 Framing Language

One of the ways that your intellectual environment and your world view expresses itself is in the use of framing language. These are the **words, phrases, metaphors, symbols, definitions, grammatical structures, questions, and so on which we use to think and speak of things in a certain way**. We frame things by describing or defining them with certain interpretations in mind. We also frame things by the way we place emphasis on certain words and not on others. And we frame things by interpreting and responding selectively to things said by others.

As an example, think of some of the ways that people speak about their friendships and relationships. We say things like "We connected", "Let's hook up", "They're attached to each other", and "They separated". We sometimes speak of getting married as "getting hitched". These phrases borrow from the vocabulary of machine functions. And to use them is to place human relations within the frame of machine functions. Now this might be a very useful way to talk about relationships, and if so, then it is not so bad. But if for some reason you need to think or speak of a relationship differently, then you may need to invent a new framing language with which to talk about it. And if this is the only framing language you've ever used to talk about relationships, it might be extremely difficult for you to think about relationships any other way.

As a thought experiment, see if you can invent a framing language for your friendships and relationships based on something else. Try using a framing language based on cooking, or travel, or music, or house building, as examples.

Here's another example of the use of framing language. Consider the following two statements:

"In the year 1605, Guy Fawkes attempted to start a people's revolution against corruption, inherited privilege, and social injustice in the British government."

"In the year 1605, Guy Fawkes planned a terrorist attack against against a group of Protestant politicians, in an attempt to install a Catholic theocracy in Britain."

Both of these statements, taken as statements of fact, are true. But they are both framed very differently. In the first statement, Fawkes is portrayed as a courageous political activist. In the second, he is framed (!) as a dangerous religious fanatic. And because of the different frames, they lead the reader to understand and interpret the man's life and purposes very differently. This, in turn, leads the reader to draw different conclusions.

In other situations, the use of framing language can have serious economic or political consequences. Consider, as an example, the national debate that took place in the United States over the Affordable Health Care Act of 2009. The very name of the legislation itself framed the discussion in the realm of market economics: the word 'affordable' already suggests that the issue has to do with money. And most people who participated in that national debate, including supporters and opponents and everything in between, spoke of health care as if it is a kind of market commodity, which can be bought or sold for a price. The debate thus became primarily a matter of questions like who will pay for it (the state? individuals? insurance companies?), and whether the price is fair. But there are other ways to talk about health care besides the language of economics. Some people frame heath care as a human right. Some frame it as a form of organized human

compassion, and some as a religious duty. But once the debate had been framed in the language of market economics, these other ways of thinking about health care were mostly excluded from the debate itself.

As noted earlier, it's probably not possible to speak about anything without framing it one way or another. But your use of framing language can limit or restrict the way things can be thought of and spoken about. They can even prevent certain ways of thinking and speaking. And when two or more people conversing with each other frame their topic differently, some unnecessary conflict can result, just as if they were starting from different premises or presupposing different world views. So it can be important to monitor one's own words, and know what frame you are using, and whether that frame is assisting or limiting your ability to think and speak critically about a particular issue. It can also be important to listen carefully to the framing language used by others, especially if a difference between their framing language and yours is creating problems.

And speaking of problems: this leads us to the point where the process of critical thinking begins.

1.4 Problems

Usually, logic and critical thinking skills are invoked in response to a need. And often, this need takes the form of a **problem** which can't be solved until you gather some kind of information. Sometimes the problem is practical: that is, it has to do with a specific situation in your everyday world.

For example:

- Perhaps you have an unusual illness and you want to recover as soon as possible.
- Perhaps you are an engineer and your client wants you to build something you've never built before.
- Perhaps you just want to keep cool on a very hot day and your house doesn't have an air conditioner.

The problem could also be theoretical: in that case, it has to do with a more general issue which impacts your whole life altogether, but perhaps not any single separate part of it in particular. Religious and philosophical questions tend to be theoretical in this sense.

For example:

- You might have a decision to make which will change the direction of your life irreversibly.
- You might want to make up your mind about whether God exists.
- You might be mourning the death of a beloved friend.
- You might be contemplating whether there is special meaning in a recent unusual dream.
- You might be a parent and you are considering the best way to raise your children.

The philosopher Karl Jaspers described a special kind of problem, which he thought was the origin of philosophical thinking. He called this kind of problem a *Grenzsituationen*, or a "**limit situation**".

> Limit situations are moments, usually accompanied by experiences of dread, guilt or acute anxiety, in which the human mind confronts the restrictions and pathological narrowness of its existing forms, and allows itself to abandon the securities of its limitedness, and so to enter new realm of self-consciousness. [3]

In other words, a limit situation is a situation in which you meet something in the world that is unexpected and surprising. It is a situation that more or less forces you to acknowledge that your way of thinking about the world so far has been very limited, and that you have to find new ways to think about things in order to solve your problems and move forward with your life. This acknowledgement, according to Jaspers, produces anxiety and dread. But it also opens the way to new and (hopefully!) better ways of thinking about things.

In general, a limit situation appears when something happens to you in your life that you have never experienced before, or which you have experienced very rarely. It might be a situation in which a long-standing belief you have held up until now suddenly shows itself to have no supporting evidence, or that the consequences of acting upon it turn out very differently than expected. You may encounter a person from a faraway culture whose beliefs are very different from yours, but whom you must regularly work with at your job, or around your neighbourhood. You may experience a crisis event in which you are at risk of death. A limit situation doesn't have to be the sort of experience that provokes a nervous breakdown or a crisis of faith, nor does it have to be a matter of life and death. But it does tend to be the type of situation in which your usual and regular habits of thinking just can't help you. It can also be a situation in which you have to make a decision of some kind, which doesn't necessarily require you to change your beliefs, but which you know will change your life in a non-trivial way.

1.5 Observation

Thus far, we have noted the kinds problems that tend to get thinking started, and the background in which thinking takes place. Now we can get on to studying thinking itself. In the general introduction, I wrote that clear critical thinking involves a process. The first stage of that process is *observation*.

When observing your problem, and the situation in which it appears, try to be as **objective** as possible. Being objective, here, means **being without influence from personal feelings, interests, biases, or expectations, as much as possible**. It means observing the situation as an uninvolved and disinterested third-person observer would see it. (By 'disinterested' here, I mean a person who is curious about the situation but who has no personal stake in what is happening; someone who is neither benefitted nor harmed as the situation develops.) Although it might be impossible to be totally, completely, and absolutely objective, still it certainly is possible to be objective *enough* to understand a situation as clearly and as completely as needed in order to make a good decision.

When you are having a debate with someone it is often very easy, and tempting, to simply accuse your opponent of being **biased**, and therefore in no position to understand something properly or make

21

decisions. If someone is truly biased about a certain topic, it is rational to doubt what someone says about that topic. But having grounds for reasonable doubt is not the same as having evidence that a proposition is false. Moreover, having an opinion, or a critical judgment about something, or a world view, is not the same as having a bias. Let us define a bias here as **the holding of a belief or a judgment about something even after evidence of the weakness or the faultiness of that judgment has been presented**. We will see more about this when we discuss Value Programs. For now, just consider the various ways in which we can eliminate bias from one's observations as much as possible. Here are a few examples:

- Take stock of how clearly you can see or hear what is going on. Is something obstructing your vision? Is it too bright, or too dark? Are there other noises nearby which make it hard for you to hear what someone is saying?
- Describe your situation in words, and as much as possible use value-neutral words in your description. Make no statement in your description about whether what is happening is good or bad, for you or for anyone else. Simply state as clearly as possible what is happening. If you cannot put your situation into words, then you will almost certainly have a much harder time understanding it objectively, and reasoning about it.
- Describe, also, how your situation makes you feel. Is the circumstance making you feel angry, sad, elated, fearful, disgusted, indignant, or worried? Has someone said something that challenges your world view? Your own emotional responses to the situation is part of what is 'happening'. And these too can be described in words so that we can reason about them later.
- Also, observe your instincts and intuitions. Are you feeling a 'pull', so to speak, to do something or not do something in response to the situation? Are you already calculating or predicting what is likely to happen next? Put these into words as well.
- Using numbers can often help make the judgment more objective. Take note of anything in the situation that can be counted, or measured mathematically: times, dates, distances, heights, shapes, angles, sizes, monetary values, computer bytes (kilobytes, megabytes, etc.), and so on.

- Take note of where your attention seems to be going. Is anything striking you as especially interesting or unusual or unexpected?
- If your problem is related to some practical purpose, take note of everything you need to know in order to fulfill that purpose. For instance, if your purpose is to operate some heavy machinery, and your problem is that you've never used that machine before, take note of the condition of the safety equipment, and the signs of wear and tear on the machine itself, and who will be acting as your "spotter", and so on.
- If other people are also observing the situation with you, consult with them. Share your description of the situation with them, and ask them to share their description with you. Find out if you can see what they are seeing, and show them what you are seeing. Also, try to look for the things that they might be missing.

Separating your observations from your judgments and opinions can often be difficult. But the more serious the problem, the more important it can be to observe something non-judgmentally, *before* coming to a decision. With that in mind, here's a short exercise: which of the following are observations, and which are judgments? Or, are some of them a bit of both?

- That city bus has too many people on it.
- The letter was delivered to my door by the postman at 10:30 AM.
- The two of them were standing so close to each other that they must be lovers.
- The clothes she wore suggested she probably came from a very rich family.
- The kitchen counter looked like it had been recently cleaned.
- He was swearing like a sailor.
- The old television was too heavy for him to carry.
- There's too much noise coming from your room, and it's driving me crazy!
- The latest James Bond film was a lot of fun.
- The latest James Bond film earned more than $80 million in its first week.
- I hate computers!

22

- The guy who delivered the pizza pissed me off because he was late.

1.6 Questions

Perhaps more than the problems do, good questions get the mind thinking as well. Questions express doubts, identify problems, call for solutions and demand answers. Indeed we might not fully understand the nature of a given problem until we have asked a decent question about it. Moreover, the best answers to one's questions tend to become ideas, beliefs, propositions, theories, arguments and world views. These, in turn, guide our lives and our choices in numerous ways. But some kinds of questions are better than others, and it can be important to discern the differences between them.

Good questions are:

1. TENACIOUS. We cannot easily put them away or ignore them.

2. DIRECT. They address the actual problem that you are facing, and not a tangential or unrelated issue.

3. SEARCHING. When you pose a good question, you don't already know the answer. You might have a rough or vague idea of what the answer might be, but you don't know for sure yet, and you are committed to finding out. Or, you might have several possible answers, and you want to find out whether any of them are good answers, or which one is the best.

4. SYSTEMATIC. Although you don't have a clear answer to your question, still your question is associated with a method or a plan, even if only a loose one, with which you can search for an answer. In other words: even when you don't know the answer, you still know what you're doing, and you're not scrambling in the dark. You have an idea where to look for an answer. And you are covering every place where a useful answer could be found, leaving nothing out.

5. USEFUL. The process of answering a good question actually helps you solve your problem.

6. OPEN. There might be more than one possible correct answer. (There can also be more than one possible wrong answer.) With several good answers

to your question, you may have to do a lot more work to find which of them is the best one, if your circumstance requires you to pick just one answer. But that work is ultimately very useful, and almost always leads us to better quality answers.

7. FERTILE. Some of the better answers to the question prompt more good questions. In this way, good questions can keep the mind active.

8. CONTROVERSIAL. A good question is often one which addresses itself to beliefs, ideas, ways of living, etc., which people normally take for granted. It may even be a question that no one else or very few others are asking. This does not necessarily mean that the questioner is being aggressive or confrontational. It should still be a searching question, and a direct question, and so on. But with a controversial question, the questioner often places herself at odds, in some way, with those who are committed to the beliefs being questioned, or who might not want the question asked at all. Indeed a controversial question can sometimes place the questioner in some danger by the very act of asking it. That danger might be social: by asking the question, she might risk being cold-shouldered or ostracized by her friends. Or it might be physical: by asking the question, she might place herself at odds against politically or economically powerful people and institutions, such as the law or one's employer.

The more of these qualities that a question has, the better a question it is. There are also several kinds of bad questions. Here are a few examples:

RHETORICAL QUESTIONS. This is a question in which the questioner already knows the answer, and is trying to prompt that same answer from his or her listeners. Although rhetorical questions can be interesting and perfectly appropriate in poems or storytelling, in a nonfiction text or in a more 'straight talk' conversation they are stylistically weak. Rhetorical questions are often plain statements of belief or of fact merely phrased in the form of a question. So it is generally better to state the belief or the fact directly as a proposition. Also, it's always possible that someone else will answer the rhetorical question in an unexpected

23

way. Rhetorical questions can also be used as forms of verbal aggression. They position the questioner as the controller of the debate, and they place others on the defensive, and make it harder for them to contribute to the debate as an equal.

LEADING QUESTIONS. These are questions that are designed to manipulate someone into believing something that they may or may not otherwise believe. Normally, leading questions come in a series, and the series is designed to make someone predisposed to respond to the last question in the series in a particular way. Leading questions are often used in a form of political campaigning called 'push polling' (to be discussed in the chapter on Reasonable Doubt).

LOADED OR COMPLEX QUESTIONS. A loaded question is one that cannot be given a straight answer unless the person answering it accepts a proposition that he or she might not want to accept. (More discussion of this kind of question appears in the chapter on Fallacies.) Like rhetorical questions, loaded questions can also be used aggressively, to control a debate and to subordinate the other contributors.

OBSTRUCTIONIST QUESTIONS. This is the kind of question that someone asks in order to interrupt someone else's train of thought. Obstructionist questions often look like good questions, and in a different context they may be perfectly reasonable. But the obstructionist question is designed distract a discussion away from the original topic, and prevent the discussion from reaching a new discovery or a clear decision. Typically, the obstructionist question asks about definitions, or pushes the discussion into a very abstract realm. It may also involve needlessly hair-splitting the meaning of certain words. In this sense an obstructionist question is much like the fallacy of 'red herring'. As an example, someone might obstruct a discussion of whether same-sex couples should be allowed to marry by saying: "Well, that all depends on what you mean by 'marriage'. What is marriage, anyway?"

FRAMING QUESTIONS. The framing question uses specific words, terms, and phrases to limit the way a certain topic can be discussed. There's probably no such thing as a question that doesn't frame the answers that flow from it, even if only in a small way. But it is possible to 'cook' or to 'rig' a question such that the only direct answers are ones which remain within a certain limited field of assumptions, or within a certain limited world view. Framing questions may even share some of the qualities of good questions: they might allow more than one answer, or they might open the way to further questions. But they are also like loaded questions in that they presuppose a certain way of thinking or talking about the topic, and you can't give a straight answer unless you reply within the bounds of that way of thinking and talking.

EMPTY QUESTIONS. A question is empty when it has no answer. Sometimes people will declare a question to be empty when in fact it is 'open': but a question with more than one possible good answer is not an empty question. So it is important to understand the difference between the two. A question is empty when all its answers lead to dead ends: when, for instance, the best answers are neither true nor false, or when different answers are nothing more than different descriptions of the same situation, or when the question cannot be given a direct answer at all. Such questions might be interesting for artistic or religious or similar purposes, and they can be the basis for some beautiful poems and meditations, or some very enjoyable comedy. But reasoning about such questions in a logical or systematic way doesn't produce any new discoveries. An empty question cannot tell you anything you don't already know.

By the way: when you are trying to observe a situation as objectively as possible before making a decision about it, you can also try to observe the way other people are talking about it. What kind of questions are they asking? What kind of framing language are they using in their descriptions? This, too, is part of the first stage in the process of reasoning.

And before moving on: there are things you should look for in a good answer to a good question. One of those things is that a good answer can be expressed in the form of a proposition. But we will see more about propositions a little later on.

1.7 Differing World Views

Perhaps the most difficult things to observe and question are your own beliefs. So let's look at how to do exactly that.

Once in a while, you are going to encounter differences between your world view and the intellectual environment in which you live. And you are also likely to encounter differences between your world view and other people's world views, and differences in the intellectual environments of different religions, political arrangements and cultures. And in some of those situations, you will not be able to just stand back and 'live and let live'. A judgment may have to be made, for instance about which world view you are personally prepared to live by, or which one you will support with your money or your votes or your actions in your community. You are also going to occasionally discover places where your world view doesn't "work", that is, places where it clearly does not help you understand the world, nor do what you want it to do.

Remember, you probably subscribe to several world views at the same time, some religious, some political, some cultural, some philosophical or scientific. In fact you probably subscribe to two or three world views at the same time, without consciously realizing it. Again, there's nothing wrong with that: we probably wouldn't be able to think about anything if we didn't have one.

But not all world views are created the same. Some are problematic, whether in great or small ways. Some are seriously faulty. If some part of your world view is faulty, this can muddle your thinking, and create conflict between you and other people. Thus it is very important to learn to tell the difference between a faulty world view and an acceptable one.

Some world views are faulty because **their ideas concerning the nature of the world have been proven wrong through scientific discovery**, such as the Ptolemaic model of the solar system, the 'four elements' theory of matter or the 'four humours' theory of medicine. Others are faulty because **their political and moral consequences have turned out to be very destructive**. Mediaeval feudalism, Soviet communism,

Nazism, racism, sexism, and prejudice, are the best-known examples of morally faulty world views. Some world views that are deeply faulty may have one or two features that seem very appealing and plausible. The way the sun rises in the east and sets in the west certainly makes it look as if the earth is standing still and the sun is traveling around it, as the Ptolemaic world view suggests. The 'four humours' theory of medicine seems to correspond elegantly to the 'four elements' theory of matter. Under Soviet communism, from Stalin's time in the early 1940's until the fall of the Berlin Wall in 1989, nobody was unemployed. And in Nazi Germany, productive and high-achieving workers could receive a free holiday trip, paid for by the government. But these apparent benefits should not blind you to the moral and empirical failures of a faulty world view.

Schweitzer described three properties that he thought **an acceptable world view** had to have. In his view, an acceptable world view had to be: **rational**, **ethical**, and **optimistic**. Let's see how Schweitzer explains each of these points in turn.

First, an acceptable world view is rational when it is the product of a lot of careful thinking about the way things really are.

> "Only what has been well turned over in the thought of the many, and thus recognised as truth, possesses a natural power of conviction which will work on other minds and will continue to be effective. Only where there is a constant appeal to the need of a reflective view of things are all man's spiritual capacities called into activity." (Schweitzer, ibid pg. 86-7.)

This is stipulated in order that the world view may help people come to an understanding of the world and of one another. A world-view derived from unreflective instincts and impulses, in his view, cannot properly reflect reality, nor will it have sufficient power to motivate people to take action when they should.

Now, Schwitzer's words in that quotation might seem very circular. It may look as if he's saying 'a world view is rational when it's rational'. But what I suspect Schweitzer had in mind is something like this. A

25

world view is rational when lots of people examine it carefully and critically, and in so doing, they determine whether or not it is actually able to explain things. Thus an acceptably rational world view **corresponds appropriately and usefully to the world as people actually experience it**. In that sense, a rational world view is a highly realistic one.

Second, an acceptable world view is ethical when it can tell us something about the difference between right and wrong, and when it can help us become better human beings.

26

> "Ethics is the activity of man directed to secure the inner perfection of his own personality... From the ethical comes ability to develop the purposive state of mind necessary to produce action on the world and society, and to cause the co-operation of all our achievements to secure the spiritual and moral perfection of the individual which is the final end of civilization."
> (ibid pg. 94-5)

It's important to note here that when Schweitzer speaks of a world view as 'ethical', he is not saying that an acceptable world view has to include certain specific moral statements. He is not saying, for example, that an ethically acceptable world view must be Christian, or that it must be Liberal, or whatever. Rather, he is saying that it has to have *something* to say about what is right or wrong, and *something* to say about how we can become better human beings, *whatever that something might be*. One world view might say that it is always wrong to harm animals, for instance. Another might say it can be right to harm animals under certain conditions. A third might claim that it is never wrong to harm animals. The point is not that one of these three possibilities is acceptable and the others aren't. The point is that all three of them are robust propositions about morality, regardless of whether you agree or disagree with them. Thus all three of those examples can be part of an acceptable world view.

It can often be tempting to say that a world view is unacceptable or invalid because it asserts moral claims that you find disagreeable. Doing so can make you look strong-willed and more certain of your values. But

it can also create unnecessary conflict with others who are just as strongly committed to their own different world views. Remember, it is possible to acknowledge that a world view is 'acceptable' in Schweitzer's sense, while at the same time disagreeing with it.

Schweitzer's third criteria for an acceptable world view is that it must be optimistic. By this he means that it must presuppose that life on earth is valuable and good.

> "That theory of the universe is optimistic which gives existence the preference as against non-existence and thus affirms life as something possessing value in itself. From this attitude to the universe and to life results the impulse to raise existence, in so far as our influence can affect it, to its highest level of value. Thence originates activity directed to the improvement of the living conditions of individuals, of society, of nations and of humanity." (Schweitzer, ibid, pp. 93-4)

Overall, according to Schweitzer, a world view that is not rational, not optimistic, and not ethical, whether in whole or in part, is (to that extent) a problematic or a faulty world view.

1.8 Value Programs

One important type of faulty world view is the kind which Canadian philosopher John McMurtry called a "value program". Value programs are world views which have the following two qualities:

- There's at least one proposition about values that cannot be questioned under any circumstances or for any reason, even when there is evidence available which shows that the proposition is weak, open to reasonable doubt, or even clearly false.
- Acting on the unquestionable proposition, and behaving and making choices as if that proposition is true, tends to cause a lot of preventable harm to people, or to their environments.

Here are McMurtry's own words, to describe what value programs are like:

In the pure-type case, which will be our definition of a value program, all people enact its prescriptions and functions as presupposed norms of what they all ought to do. All assume its value designations and value exclusions as givens. They seek only to climb its ladder of available positions to achieve their deserved reward as their due. Lives are valued, or not valued, in terms of the system's differentials and measurements. All fulfill its specified roles without question and accept its costs, however widespread, as unavoidable manifestations of reality. In the strange incoherence of the programmed mind, the commands of the system are seen as both freely chosen and as laws of nature, or God… Those who are harmed by the value program are ignored, or else blamed for falling on its wrong side, because its rule is good and right. Its victims must, it is believed, be at fault. A value program's ideology is in great part devoted to justifying the inevitability of the condition of the oppressed. [4]

McMurtry added to his discussion that world views become value programs not due to a fault in human nature, but rather due to a kind of social or psychological conditioning: "…it is not "human nature" that is the problem. The problem is not in how we are constructed, but in the inert repetition of the mind, a condition that does not question socially conditioned value programs." [5]

It's usually easy to identify value programs from history: mediaeval feudalism, for instance. But perhaps the more important questions are:

- What are the value programs of our time?
- Are you, or the people around you, unknowingly subscribing to a value program?
- Are there propositions in your intellectual environment which cannot be questioned, or which can be questioned but only at great personal risk?
- Is anyone harmed through the ways you live your life in accordance with the teachings of your world view? How are those harms explained? And are those explanations justifiable? Why or why not?
- In what ways, if at all, does your world view meet, or fail to meet, Schweitzer's three criteria for acceptability?

As an exercise, have a look at this short list of world views of our time, and think about whether any of them are value programs, and why (or why not):

- Representative parliamentary democracy.
- Free-market capitalism.
- Human rights.
- The 'trickle-down' theory of economics.
- The right to bear arms.
- The pro-choice movement.
- The pro-life movement.
- Manifest Destiny.
- The 'fandom' of any professional sports team.
- The official platform of any major political party.
- The teachings, doctrines, and creeds of any major religion.

1.9 World Views, Civilization, and Conflict

In 1993, American historian and political scientist Samuel Huntington published a paper called "A Clash of Civilizations?" In that paper he defined 'civilization' as "the highest cultural grouping of people and the broadest level of cultural identity people have short of that which distinguishes humans from other species." [6] The idea here is like this. Think of the biggest grouping of people that you feel part of, such that the only grouping of people that is larger than that one is the human race as a whole. You will probably find yourself thinking about more than just your country or your religion, or those who speak the same language as you. Rather, you will find yourself thinking of people who share a few simple concepts in their world views, even while they live in different countries or speak different languages. With this definition in mind, Huntington thought that there are nine civilizations active in the world right now: Western, Latin American, Slavic, Middle Eastern, African, Hindu, Chinese, Buddhist, and Japanese. Huntington also thought that some countries, such as Ethiopia, and Turkey, are 'torn' countries. In a torn country, some forces in that country are working to transition the country from one civilization to another, while at the same time other forces in the same country resist that transition.

27

4 McMurtry, "Unequal Freedoms" (Garamond, 1998) pg. 6

5 Ibid

6 Huntington, "A Clash of Civilisations?" Foreign Affairs,

Summer 1993

Huntington further argued that differences in world view and civilization are going to be the basis for all future armed conflict.

"…the fundamental source of conflict in this new world will not be primarily ideological or primarily economic. The great divisions among humankind and the dominating source of conflict will be cultural. Nation states will remain the most powerful actors in world affairs, but the principal conflicts of global politics will occur between nations and groups of different civilizations." (Huntington, ibid.)

Finally, Huntington also gives a particular privilege to religion. In his view, economic globalisation has had the effect of reducing the importance of the nation-state in shaping and defining personal identity. Religion, he says, has taken its place, since religion "… provides a basis for identity and commitment that transcends national boundaries and unites civilizations." (*ibid.*)

The important question here, of course, is whether or not Huntington's claim about the inevitability of conflict is correct.

1.10 Exercise for Chapter One: How Much Variety Is In Your World?

I have more than one thousand people on my Facebook list. So I see lot of "memes" every day. Memes are ideas, expressed in pictures and videos and quotations and so on, which people share with each other, and the more they are shared the more their movements seem to take on a life of their own. One day I thought it would be fun to save them to a database, and tag them according to the kind of messages they express. What would I discover? Were there some kinds of memes that are more popular than others? What are these things really telling me about the thoughts and feelings of the people around me? And what are they telling me about myself?

The original idea was to take a kind of "snapshot" of the content of my (online) intellectual environment over four days to see what was in it. My basic rules

were simple. I would take only the pictures which appeared while I happened to be online. That way, I wouldn't have to be online all day. And I also promised myself not to deliberately change my web surfing habits during those days, so that I wouldn't get an artificial result. I also didn't track the links to blog posts, news articles, videos, or other online media. Just to be simple, I only tracked the photos and images. And I only tracked the ones that someone on my list shared after having seen it elsewhere. That way, each of these pictures had passed a kind of natural selection test. Someone had created the image and passed it on to someone who thought it worthy of being passed on to a third person.

After the first few hours, I had about 50 memes for my collection. And I already noticed a few general trends. So I started tagging the samples into what appeared to be the four most obvious categories: Inspirational, Humorous, Political, and Everything Else. The Humour category was already by far the largest, with more samples than the other categories combined. At the end of the first day, there was enough variety in the collection that I could create sub-categories. The largest of which was "Humour involving cats or kittens". No surprise there, I suppose.

But at the end of the second day, with about 200 samples in my collection, I started to notice something else, which was much more interesting. A small but significant number of these samples had to with social, political, or religious causes other than those that I personally support. Some promoted causes that were reasonably similar to my values, but I have never done all that much to support them. For instance, I've nothing against vegetarianism, but I'm not vegetarian myself. So I labeled those ones the "near" values, because they are not my values, but they are reasonably close, and I felt no sense of being in conflict with them. Then I noticed that some of my samples were for causes almost directly opposed to the ones I normally support. So instead of "un-friending" people with different political views than me, I saved and tracked their political statements just as I did everybody else's. And I labeled those statements the "far" values, because they expressed values fairly distant from my own.

28

So now I could look at all these images and put them in three broad groups: Common values, Near values, and Far values. And in doing so, I had discovered a way to statistically measure the real variety of my intellectual environment, and the extent to which I am actually exposed to seriously different world views. Let's name this measurement your 'Intellectual Environment Diversity Quotient'. Or, to be short about it, your 'DQ'.

At the end of four days, I had 458 pictures, and I had tagged them into six broad categories: Inspirational, Humour, Religion, Causes, Political, and Foreign Language. Here's how it all turned out. (Note here that if some of these numbers don't seem to add up, that is because some samples were tagged more than once, as they fit into two or (rarely) three categories.)

TOTAL SIZE OF THE DATASET: 458 (100.0%)
Inspirational images: 110 (24.0%) *Humour:* 225 (49.1%) *Religion:* 36 (7.8%) *Causes:* 148 (32.3%) *Political:* 47 (10.2%) *Foreign language:* 11 (2.4%)

And by the way, only 5 of them asked the recipient to "like" or "share" the image.

Now, for the sake of calculating how much real difference there is in my intellectual environment, we have to look at just the images expressing social, political, religious, or philosophical values of some kind. This doesn't necessarily exclude the inspirational or comic pictures that had some kind of political or moral message, because as mentioned, a lot of the pictures got more than one tag. As it turned out, around half of them were making statements about values. (That, by the way, was also very interesting.)

Here's the breakdown of exactly what my friends were posting pictures about. And as you can see, there's a lot of variety. But what is interesting is not how different they are from each other. What's interesting is how many of them are different from my own point of view. You can figure this for yourself by comparing the memes in your own timeline to what you say about yourself in your own FB profile, or by just deciding with each image, one at a time, how far you agree or

disagree with each one. But in either case you have to be really honest with yourself. In this way, calculating your DQ is not just about taking a snapshot of your intellectual environment. It's also about knowing yourself, and making a few small but serious decisions about what you really stand for.

TOTAL RELIGION, CAUSES, & POLITICAL:
231 (100.0%)

TOTAL RELIGIOUS: 36 (15.5%)
Buddhism: 4 (1.7%) *Christianity:* 6 (2.5%) *Pagan:* 8 (3.4%) *Northern / Asatru:* 6 (2.5%) *Aboriginal / First Nations:* 3 (1.2%) *Taoism:* 1 (0.4%) *Hindu:* 1 (0.4%) *Any:* 6 (2.5%) *Atheism:* 1 (0.4%)

TOTAL CAUSES: 148 (64.0%)
Against cruelty to animals: 3 (1.2%) *Against religious proselytization:* 3 (1.2%) *Support education, science, critical thinking:* 19 (8.2%) *Pro-vegetarian:* 1 (0.4%) *Organic and/or backyard gardening:* 3 (1.2%) *Feminism / anti-violence against women:* 3 (1.2%) *Feminism / sexual power relations:* 7 (3.0%) *Feminism / body image:* 5 (2.1%) *Anti-war:* 4 (1.7%) *Israel-Iran antiwar solidarity:* 3 (1.2%) *Support for soldiers / war veterans:* 8 (3.4%) *Support for retired military dogs:* 2 (0.8%) *Support gun ownership:* 3 (1.2%) *Race relations, anti racism:* 1 (0.4%) *Support gay marriage / LGBT pride:* 10 (4.3%) *Support environmentalism:* 5 (2.1%) *Support universal health care in America:* 1 (0.4%) *Support the student protest in Quebec:* 3 (1.2%) *Against fascism and Neo-Nazism:* 1 (0.4%)

TOTAL PARTY POLITICAL: 47 (20.3%)
Right wing: 8 (3.4%) *Left wing:* 36 (15.5%) *Centre:* 3 (1.2%)

Now for the sake of figuring your DQ, we need to look at the percentage of value-expressing memes that are near to my values, and the percentage of those which are distant. That's the measure of how much of the intellectual environment you live in could really challenge you, if you let it.

29

Total: 231 / 100.0%
Common values = 150 / 64.9%
Near values = 64 / 27.7%
Far values = 17 / 7.3%
So, my DQ, rounded off, is **28** and **7**.

Now, you might be thinking, if I did the experiment on a different day, I'd collect different samples, and I'd get a different result. This was especially clear in the humorous pictures, because some of them depended on the time of year for their effect. For example, I got a lot of Douglas Adams references, because one of the days I was collecting the images was "Towel Day". I also got a lot of Star Wars images because I was collecting my samples on May the 4th. Similar effects can also influence the memes that were expressing values, for instance if the dataset is collected during a religious holiday. Therefore, the figure I just quoted above might not be very accurate. Well, to address that possibility, I ran the experiment again two weeks later. And here's what I got the second time.

Second set = 470
Total Religion, Causes, Political, Second Set: 243 (100.0%)
Common values = 157 (64.6%)
Near values = 77 (31.6%)
Far values = 9 (3.7%)

As you can see, it's a slightly different result. The total collection was larger, and there were a lot fewer distant values represented. And among the comic pictures, there were a lot more references to Doctor Who. But overall it wasn't a big difference. In fact the fraction of pictures which expressed some kind of value was still about 50%, just as before. So if I add the second set to the first, and do the math again, I can get a more accurate result, like this:

Both sets combined = 474 (100.0%)
Common values = 307 (64.7%)
Near values = 141 (29.7%)
Far values = 26 (5.4%)
New DQ = **30** and **4**.

Now, I don't know whether that figure is high or low, because I have no one else's data to compare it to. And I also don't know whether it would be good or bad to have a high DQ, or a low one, because, well, that's a value statement too!

But what I do know is that I can now accurately measure the extent to which my intellectual environment has a real range of different ideas and opinions. I can measure how much "otherness", social or religious or political "other-ness", exists in my world. I can also measure how much I prefer the somewhat less stressful company of people who think more or less the same way I do. Or, I can also measure the extent to which my intellectual environment serves only as a kind of echo-chamber, repeating back to me my own ideas without examining them very deeply.

But the really fun part of this experiment is that you can do it too! What's your DQ?

30

Curiosity, Self-Awareness,
Health, Courage, Healthy
Skepticism, Autonomy,
Simplicity, Precision, Patience

———————————————————

Self-Interest, Saving Face,
Peer Pressure, Stereotyping,
Prejudice, Skepticism,
Intellectual Laziness, Relativism

Chapter Two: Habits of Good and Bad Thinking

We have seen some of the problems that can arise when different world views and different intellectual environments come into conflict with each other. Now let us look at some of the problems that can arise when a given world view comes into conflict with *itself*. There are various ways that people think, and various ways people pull their world views together, which actually make it harder for people to find the truth about anything, communicate with each other effectively, and solve their problems. And there are other ways people think which make it easier to communicate, solve problems, and discover truths. I shall call these things 'good and bad thinking habits'.

Note that I call these principles of thinking 'habits' rather than rules. This is because there are various exceptions to each of them. There can occasionally be situations in which a good thinking habit might be inappropriate, or in which a bad thinking habit might be very useful. But such exceptions tend to be very rare. You will almost always be thinking rationally and clearly when your thinking follows the good habits and avoids the bad habits.

The bad habits tend to arise in two ways. They arise because of **how we think**: these bad habits are mostly psychological factors such as fears, motivations, and attitudes. Bad habits also arise because of **what we think**: these habits arise when our thinking involves problematic beliefs. Again, thinking in terms of such bad habits are not signs that one's thinking is *necessarily* or *inevitably* wrong. (In this way, they are different from the fallacies, which we will discuss later on.) They do, however, tend to make one's thinking very

weak, and very vulnerable to criticism and objection. They also tend to make one's views and beliefs easily manipulated by other people. When they form a prominent part of one's intellectual environment, they tend to introduce faults into one's world view.

2.1.1 Self-Interest

On its own, self interest need not be a bad thing. Most people make decisions at least in part on the basis of what they think will benefit them. Self-interest can be a problem when you advance some argument or defend some world view only because you personally stand to benefit if it's true, and for no other reason.

The notion of self-interest has an important place in some specialized forms of reasoning, such as game theory and economics. We find it in sources as ancient as Aristotle: his claim that everyone by nature desires happiness was the starting place for his theory of ethics. We find it in the work of John Stuart Mill, who made the pursuit of 'utility', meaning pleasure or personal benefit, the basis of his theory of ethics, called Utilitarianism. Adam Smith, widely regarded as 'the father of modern economics', also placed self-interest at the centre of his work. To Smith, self-interest was a normal part of rational human behaviour, and often a very self-defeating kind of behaviour. But in a properly functioning economy, Smith reasoned, businesspeople and investors would direct their self-interest toward public goods.

Self-interest also plays an important part in a branch of mathematics called game theory. Without going into a lot of detail about each of these writers and others who were like them, let it suffice to say that self-interest is a very powerful psychological force in people's minds. All the writers mentioned here are very careful to specify the ways in which self-interest is rational and useful, and the ways in which it is irrational and even damaging. For this reason, some logicians prefer to separate 'intelligent self interest' from ordinary selfishness and egotism. Intelligent self-interest looks for the 'bigger picture', sees the ways in which one's own interests can align with other people's interests, is willing to sacrifice short-term benefits for the sake of longer-term benefits, and recognizes that some kinds of benefits or advantages for the self are not really worth pursuing.

Self-interest tends to get in the way of good reasoning when people have a strong emotional or economic stake in something that looks like it might be under threat from others. In such situations, people tend to get passionate and emotional, and this almost always clouds their judgments. If you secretly want something to be true, and you stand to benefit from it being true (for instance, if you might make money that way), but there's little or no reason for it to be true, you may inadvertently misinterpret the evidence, or discount contradictory evidence, or invent rationalizations that have little or no logical strength. This can lead you to a faulty understanding of your situation, and as a result you are more likely to make bad decisions.

2.1.2 Saving Face

Among the various ways that people are self-interested, most people are also interested in having a good reputation, and being liked or even admired by others around them. No one, or almost no one, enjoys having their faults, weaknesses, harmful actions, or foolish choices pointed out to them by others. Moreover nobody, or almost nobody, likes to be proven wrong by others. And this, by itself, is not a bad thing. But because of this interest, people sometimes cover up their mistakes. Or, if it is shown to them that some of their ideas or beliefs are unworkable or absurd, they might continue to argue in favour of them anyway, in

order to avoid admitting that the other person might be right. When we do this, we are falling into the habit of saving face.

The habit of saving face is in some ways related to a condition described by psychologists called **"cognitive dissonance".** This is what happens when someone is confronted with, or contemplates, two or more beliefs that cannot both be true at the same time. (Especially these two contradictory thoughts: "I am a good person" and "I caused someone harm".) Most people are strongly psychologically disposed to avoid having contradictions like that in their thoughts. And most people don't like to have muddled thoughts like that pointed out to them by others: it makes us look foolish. And so people tend to invent self-interested reasons to reject one or other of the contradicting beliefs, with the real purpose of restoring their sense of self worth. But this can sometimes blind us to the truth, or even prevent people from finding out what the truth really is.

Examples:

"Only six people came to the company picnic. I was on the organizing team. But it wasn't my job to send out the invitations."

"I got an 'F' on that essay. But I'm getting an 'A' in all my other classes. Clearly, the professor doesn't know what he's doing."

"Jim has been my best friend for ten years and he's always been nice to me. So I just can't believe he is the one who stole the old man's wallet. You must be mistaken."

"Sally has been my best friend for ten years. But tonight she stole my wallet. I guess she was a bad person all along, and she just tricked me into thinking she was a good person."

2.1.3 Peer Pressure

All of us are members of various communities and social groups, as we saw in the discussion of world views and intellectual environments. Each of those groups tends to have a few prevalent ideas, practices, and beliefs, that form part of the group's identity. Here let us add that most of these groups also exert a bit of psychological pressure on the members to accept the group's prevalent ideas, practices, and beliefs. Sometimes that pressure can be very subtle, and very limited. You might get nothing more than an odd look or a cold shoulder if you say something that doesn't fit with the group's main beliefs. Other times, it might be very overt and unambiguous, and perhaps connected to threats of punishment for non-conformity. You might be shut out of the group's decision-making process, or not invited to the group's events anymore, or (if one's non-conformity is persistent) even targeted with malicious gossip or threats of violence. Thus, people tend to keep their dissenting views to themselves, or they change their views to better fit the group. Now, the ideas shared by the group might be right, or they might be wrong, or they might be somewhere in between. But the number of people who believe those ideas has nothing to do with whether those ideas are any good. Problems almost always arise when someone accepts an idea or a world view *only* because it is an idea or a world view favoured by the group he or she belongs to, and for no other reason.

2.1.4 Stereotyping and Prejudice

Since we are speaking of peer pressure: a community or social group might have a few beliefs about people who belong to other groups. The group might look up to other groups, or down upon them, or attribute some quality or behavioral trait to all of them. This becomes a bad habit when there is little or no real evidence that all members of that other group share that quality. We might build stereotypes of people based on how they are characterised in entertainment media, or on your experiences meeting one or two members of that group. But in terms of the actual evidence to support the stereotype, the 'sample size' is always too small. It's usually based on only a handful of cases, and then generalized to a massively larger group. In this way it is a case of the fallacy of hasty generalization. In fact, the

sample size can be as small as zero: some people develop stereotypes without any evidence at all. They've just been taught to think that way by their intellectual environment. Stereotyping almost always treats people as tokens of a type, almost never as individuals with their own distinct qualities. In this way, it prevents us from knowing the truth about individuals, and can even prevent us from knowing the truth about the various groups that person might belong to.

As stereotyping is the assumption that all members of a given social group are somehow basically the same; so too is prejudice a hostile or harmful judgment about the merit or the worth of people in that group, assigned on the basis of a stereotypical assumption. One of the ideas that a group might pressure its members to believe is the idea that one's own group is better than other groups. This almost always leads people to see the ideas and world views of rival groups in the very worst possible light. And it leads people to treat members of the rival group badly. Racism, sexism, religious discrimination, classism, poor-bashing, and able-ism, are all examples of this. Prejudice is also hurtful when the qualities it assigns are qualities that subordinate people or which deny them full membership in the human race. There might be a spectrum of intensity, which at one end attributes only a few relatively minor bad qualities such as foolishness or uncleanliness, and which at the other might incite strong feelings of hate or fear, such as criminality, emotional instability, animalistic physical features, disease, or even a secret conspiratorial agenda. But in any case, stereotyping and prejudice almost always prevents people from seeing things and people as they truly are.

Why do prejudiced beliefs persist? The main reason is because those beliefs are supported by peer pressure. When among prejudiced people, uttering a disparaging remark about the target group might be actually encouraged and rewarded in various ways: smiles, happy laughter, welcoming gestures, and approving words. In this way, prejudiced beliefs persist when people do not think for themselves, but rather when they allow other (prejudiced) people to do their thinking for them.

35

2.1.5. Excessive Skepticism

It is usually very healthy to be a little bit skeptical of things, and not to take things at face value all the time. Some people, however, believe that we cannot truly know anything unless we can be absolutely certain of it, and that we are beyond any possible doubt about it. That level of skepticism is almost always too much.

Excessive skepticism tends to appear when people try to estimate the riskiness of some activity. The excessively skeptical person tends to make a 'big deal' of the risks involved, and might be unwilling to do anything until he is satisfied that everything is absolutely safe and certain. Or he might be unwilling to do something because 'it's never been tried before'. But it's often the case that we have to act even in situations where success is very uncertain, and there is no way to absolutely guarantee safety. The moon landings from 1969-72 are good examples here. No one really knew whether the missions would succeed, or fail, or even end in total disaster. (At one time, astronomers thought that the dark 'seas' on the moon were made of sand, and they worried that the landing craft would sink!) The excessively skeptical person weighs the risks too heavily, and often ends up unable to act because of that skepticism. He may even try to prevent others from acting, because of his own doubts.

Excessive skepticism can also appear in matters that are almost purely theoretical. For instance, some people might doubt the reality of the world outside their own minds. It can be fun to speculate about whether or not we are being deceived by Descartes' Evil Genius, or whether we are all living inside a computer-generated virtual reality. Sometimes it can be fun to ask 'How do you know?' in an infinite regress, the way small children sometimes do.

But most of the time, we don't need to have such high standards for certainty. It is enough that one's beliefs are beyond *reasonable* doubt; they do not have to be beyond *all possible* doubt. As a rule of thumb, remember that **doubt based on speculation without evidence is not *reasonable* doubt.** It's not enough to say that something is doubtful because some alternative explanation might be possible. It's also important to say something about how probable the alternative explanation really is. If an alternative explanation is possible but very unlikely, and there isn't much evidence for it, then it isn't a good basis for skepticism. So if you dreamed last night that you ran away to a foreign country and married your worst enemy, then that 'might' be because in some parallel universe that's exactly what you did. But there's no evidence to support that possibility, so it's best to discount it as a reasonable explanation for your dream.

We shall see more about skepticism among the good thinking habits, and later on we'll see it again in the discussion of reasonable doubt.

2.1.6 Intellectual Laziness

This is the habit of "giving up too soon", or deliberately avoiding the big questions. This is the habit we indulge when we say things like: "thinking that way is too confusing," or "your questions drive me crazy", or "these questions cannot be answered, you just have to accept it". Laziness also appears when you answer a philosophical question with a witty quotation from a movie or a popular song, as if that's all that needs to be said about the topic. Some people actually go to great efforts to defend their laziness, with complex arguments for why intellectually enquiring or scientifically minded people "can't handle the mystery of things", or why they want to "take away the beauty and the magic of the world."

A variation of intellectual laziness is **willed ignorance**. This is the habit of deliberately preventing oneself from answering hard questions or acknowledging relevant facts. Some people prefer to live in a kind of bubble, where serious challenges to their world views never appear. And while it can be a sign of integrity to preserve the core values of one's world view, it is also the case that deliberately shutting out facts or realities that challenge one's world view can lead one to make poor decisions. Your world view might hold that some questions are unanswerable, or that some questions are not allowed to be asked. Similarly, you might prevent yourself from acknowledging facts or realities that could serve as evidence of the wrongness of some part of your world view. Willed ignorance actually takes some effort, and perhaps isn't precisely the same as laziness. But it has the same basic effect: it prevents people from learning things that they may need to know, and so makes it more likely that they will make bad decisions, or turn their world views into value programs.

Some people might even argue that there is no such thing as 'Truth', with a big capital T, referring to statements about the ultimate things like God, or justice, or knowledge, or reality. They might believe that it is pointless to claim that any given idea or belief or explanation of such things is true, no matter how well supported it might be by the facts or by logic. There might be an appeal to some kind of relativism as the reason for why there's no such thing as an ultimate truth. And in that sense, this line of thinking is not truly lazy: it goes to some effort to seriously defend the claim that no one can make a serious claim about such things. But the real function of such assertions is to justify a refusal to think deeply and carefully about the things that matter. It may be the case that there are, or that there are not, ultimate truths about such things. But the intellectually lazy or willfully ignorant person does none of the work needed to find out. They actually do not know, and they have made their ignorance into a kind of rule for their thinking.

It might not be polite or kind to name this habit 'laziness', but that's what it really is. Just as one can be lazy at practical tasks like cleaning your house, you can be lazy in your thinking about pressing problems or important questions. And just as laziness in your practical affairs can hurt you eventually, there are times when lazy thinking can cause you great trouble later on, too. Lazy thinking can make it easier for others to manipulate and deceive you, for instance. And it can also paralyze you into doing nothing in situations where decisions must be made.

2.1.7 Relativism

Philosophical arguments are often presented in the form of debates. Sometimes there are two positions that are opposed to each other, and each side presents arguments that support their position while showing the problems with the opposing position. Consider, as an example, a debate about the moral permissibility of the death penalty. The speakers might take these two positions:

A: The death penalty is morally permissible (for reasons x, y, z).
B: The death penalty is not morally permissible (for reasons a, b, c).

When assessing the evidence for these claims, philosophers are trying to establish whether it is true or false that the death penalty is morally permissible. In this case the moral permissibility of the death penalty is being treated like a fact. Often beginning philosophers are not comfortable with treating moral, epistemic, or aesthetic claims as being either right or wrong. Philosophical claims are not scientific claims for which we can provide empirical evidence, and often both sides provide very compelling arguments. This can make it seem as if both sides are right. Sometimes it makes sense to search for a middle ground, however, it is not always possible or desirable. It is, furthermore, a contradiction to say that the death penalty both is and is not morally permissible. When is it morally permissible? What makes the death penalty morally permissible in some cases but not others? More needs to be said.

Relativism is the view that a claim is only true or false relative to some other condition. There are many varieties of relativism: but the two most common kinds are:

- **Subjective relativism**, also known as **Personal Belief relativism**, is the claim that the truth about anything depends on what someone believes. It is the view that all truth is in the 'eye of the beholder'; or that something is true *if (and only if) someone believes it to be true*, and then it is true *for that person*, and perhaps only for that person. In ethics, subjective relativism is the idea that an action is morally right if the person doing that action believes it to be morally right. Nothing makes an action right or wrong except the judgment of the person doing it.

- **Cultural Relativism** is the idea that something is true, or right, etc., because it is generally believed to be so by some culture or society. Further, it is true, or right, etc., for *that* society.

Here we will examine relativism about truth as it pertains to philosophical claims about ethics and knowledge that you are likely to encounter in an introductory class. As relativism is very appealing to beginning philosophers, it is important to look at some different kinds of relativistic arguments, the problems with them, and some of the typical reasons for adopting a relativistic position.

One reason to adopt relativism is that philosophical claims, particularly ethical claims, can seem very subjective. With so much debate it can seem as if there are no correct answers, and that what is right or wrong can be different for different individuals. Alice believes the death penalty is okay and Barbara believes it is wrong, and who are we to tell them what to believe?

The problem with accepting this kind of relativism is that it makes a claim true or false relative to someone's beliefs, and takes beliefs to be above any justification. While it may seem arrogant to challenge other people's beliefs, examining what we take to be true and why is one of the basic components of philosophy. It isn't enough to say "Alice believes that X is okay, so X is right for her," perhaps Alice has never examined her beliefs, or came to hold them because she was given false information. Investigating what we believe and why can help us to have consistent beliefs, and also to be confident and conscientious in our ethical choices.

While it is respectful to consider others' points of view, differences in perspective does not entail that philosophical questions are entirely subjective. Learning how to carefully consider and assess reasons and justifications is part of studying philosophy. In some arguments disagreement between conclusions can mask similarities in underlying beliefs. For instance, two people can agree that murder is unjustified killing and disagree about what deaths count as murder. Alice might believe that the death penalty is state sanctioned murder, and so oppose it. Barbara might believe that a death that is sanctioned by the state is always justified. Their disagreement over the death penalty is then not only about whether it is right or wrong, but over acceptable justifications for taking someone's life.

Someone else might note that some cultures accept action X while some do not, and argue that X is morally permissible relative to culture. This is known as cultural relativism. Often students accept cultural relativism because they want to be sensitive to cultural differences. Different cultures have different practices, but can we say that a culture allowing the death penalty means it is sometimes morally permissible? There are two problems with this approach. One is that it does not allow people within a culture to disagree with the practice. If someone from culture A wants to argue against the death penalty they could not do so on moral grounds—their culture permitting it makes it a morally acceptable act. Another problem is changes in cultural practices. We want to say that slavery was abolished because people realized that it was wrong to treat people as property, not that it became immoral once the practice stopped.

There is a difference between issues that are moral and those that are social norms or matters of etiquette. In some cases it makes sense to accept cultural relativism about social practices, but in others it might seem as if some other factor, such as human rights, trumps concerns for cultural variation. It can be difficult to determine when we should and when we should not challenge the practices or beliefs of other cultures, but it requires rational inquiry and a sensitive analysis of the arguments that demands more than knee-jerk relativism.

The problems with relativism do not mean that we have to accept the view that ethical or epistemic truths are universal and absolute. There is a great deal of conceptual space between individual relativism and accepting a general moral principle. Likewise, there are ways to be culturally sensitive while challenging the practices of our own and other cultures. Some concepts that seem natural or objectively true to us may turn out to be contingent—if a culture has three rather than two concepts of gender we might reconsider why we think about gender as we do. Being open to other cultures' beliefs and attitudes can be very important to learning to see things in a different light, but it does not mean that we have to accept them without good reasons.

2.1.8 The Consequences of Bad Habits

The consequences of living with and falling into these bad thinking habits can be very serious. For instance, they can:

- Make you more vulnerable to being intimidated, bullied, or manipulated by others;
- Make you less able to stand up for yourself, or for others in need;
- Make it harder to tell the difference between truth and lies;
- Make you more dogmatic and closed-minded;
- Make you less flexible, less creative, and less ready to handle unpredictable changes in your situation.
- Lead you to justify moral decisions that needlessly harm people, including yourself;
- Lead you to suppress or ignore evidence that goes contrary to your beliefs, even if that evidence is very reliable;
- Provoke confusion or anger when presented with reasons why one's beliefs might be problematic or faulty;
- Prevent serious philosophical thinking about the most important problems in our lives;
- Prevent personal growth, maturity, and self-awareness.

With these observations in mind, let's look at some good habits.

2.2.1 Curiosity

As an intellectual habit, curiosity is the desire for knowledge. To be an intellectually curious person, you have to be the sort of person for whom the usual explanations of things are not enough to satisfy you. The curious person wants to find out more about whatever is new, strange, or interesting in the world. When something different, unusual, unexpected, or even weird and scary appear, the curious person doesn't hide from them or pretend they are other than what they are. She faces them directly, and makes an honest attempt to investigate them. And she does not settle for things to remain mysterious. Indeed part of the task of the philosopher, as it is with the scientist, is to render things un-mysterious: it is to understand things as completely as possible. Good rational thinkers love mysteries and puzzles: but they don't just stand back and "appreciate" them. They also try to figure them out.

It is precisely by being intellectually curious that good reasoning helps prevent closed minded dogmatism. Curiosity leads to discovery, invention, expanded awareness of the world, and of the self. Sometimes it leads to beauty; sometimes it leads to power. Most of all, it leads to, just as it depends on, a sense of wonder. Those who think that rationality is a set of rules for thinking which limit or constrain your experiences, or who think that rationality kills the sense of creativity and imagination, are simply wrong – and there's no polite way to say it. And it's probable that such people have actually limited their own experiences by excluding from their minds the most powerful, most inquisitive, and most successful way of knowing the world ever devised.

2.2.2 Self-Awareness

Above the entrance to the famous Oracle of Delphi, the religious centre of the classical Greek world, was written the phrase γνωθι σεατον. In English, this means 'know yourself'. The idea was that people who wanted to enter the temple should have done a sustained exercise in personal soul-searching, to be fully honest about their own individual character and habits, and also to be honest about human nature (especially human mortality).

Self-awareness involves knowing your own presuppositions, desires, biases, world views, and so on. It involves knowing your habits, faults, desires, powers, and talents. And it involves knowing something about what it means to be a thinking human being. This is a more difficult prospect than it appears to be. Some people do not find out what their own world view is until someone else says or does something which

39

challenges it. But it is an essential quality: those who do not know themselves tend to make poor decisions, and are easily manipulated by others.

2.2.3 Health

As unrelated as it may seem, taking care of your physical health is actually a good thinking habit. If you are feeling unwell, or sleep-deprived, or under stress, or for whatever reason physically uncomfortable, then it will be harder for you to observe and understand your situation, and harder to reason about it clearly. Good health, as a thinking habit, involves getting enough exercise, eating healthy real food and avoiding junk food, bathing regularly, and getting enough sleep. It also involves taking care of your mental health: and one of the simplest ways to do that is to take time every day for leisure activities that are restful.

A study conducted by psychologists in Japan found that people who gazed on forest scenery for twenty minutes produced 13.4% less salivary cortisol, a stress hormone. Walking in forests and natural settings also helped reduce high blood pressure, and reduce heart rate fluctuations. As these effects became more known, some municipalities in Japan created "forest therapy" programs for stressed-out factory workers. [7] High-stimulation activities like video games, action films, intensely athletic sports, and anything that gets your adrenaline rushing, can be a lot of fun, but they're not restful. I'm not saying you should avoid such things altogether. But good critical thinking requires calm, and peace, and quiet. To be better able to calm yourself when you need to think, give around twenty minutes or more, every day, to something genuinely relaxing, such as walking in a forest, or meditating, or reading, or cooking and eating a proper meal. Don't be multitasking at the same time. If you are experiencing a lot of frustration dealing with a certain problem, you will probably have an easier time of it after a shower, a healthy dinner, a walk in the park with a friend and a dog, and a good night's sleep.

2.2.4 Courage

Sometimes, your process of thinking about things will lead you to possibilities or conclusions that you won't like, or which your friends or associates won't like. Sometimes, you might reach a conclusion about something that might land you in trouble with your boss at work, or your teacher, your priest, your government, or anyone who has some kind of power, authority, or influence in your life. Expressing that conclusion or that thought might land you in some amount of danger: you might risk being fired from your job, or ostracized from your community. Depending on the situation, and the idea you are expressing, you might find yourself excluded, angrily criticized, ignored, arrested, imprisoned, or even killed. Even in countries where the freedom of speech and of expression and of the press is guaranteed by constitutional law, people can still run great risks by speaking their minds, even when their words are true.

Courageous thinking means thinking and expressing the dangerous thought anyway. It means **thinking and speaking without fear**. It means committing yourself to what you rationally judge to be the best conclusion, whether you like it or not, and whether your friends or your 'betters' like it or not. And this is a lot harder to do than it sounds. Strong social forces like the desire to be welcomed and included and loved, or strong institutional forces like laws or corporate policies, can lead people to keep quiet about ideas that might be controversial.

Questions and arguments can require personal courage when they challenge a very important part of one's world view. Consider the following examples:

- What if there is no god?
- What if there is no objective moral right or wrong?
- What if a very popular or charismatic person is telling half-truths or lies?
- At my workplace, am I participating in or benefitting from something unjust, or evil?
- What if life has no purpose or meaning?

---

7 Akemi Nakamura, "'Forest Therapy' taking root" The Japan Times Online, 2 May 2008

People who take such questions seriously, and who consider answers that are radically different from the answers provided by their world views, may experience a lot of self-doubt or even despair. They may find that they have to change their lives. Even the mere act of posing the questions, aside from the attempt to answer them, can land people in trouble with their friends and families. Strong social forces might pressure the questioner to not ask certain questions, or to answer them only in acceptable ways. In such situations, it can take great courage to ask such questions, and to do one's own thinking in search of a decent answer.

Questions and arguments can require public or political courage when they challenge some arrangement in your social world. It could something as simple as choosing to support a different professional sports team other than the one based in your home city, or the one supported by all your friends and family. Or, it could be something as complex and dangerous as opposing a policy of a large corporation that you work for, or which has a significant presence in the area where you live. It can take a lot of courage to criticize the actions of some entity with political power, especially when that entity can threaten people who disagree with it. If you criticize your employer, you might lose your job. If you criticize your government, you might be arrested. If you criticize your church leaders, you might be shamed, denounced, or dismissed from the church. As the philosopher Voltaire wrote, "It is dangerous to be right in matters on which the established authority is wrong."

The classical Greek language gives us a word for statements that require this kind of courage: **parrhesia**, which roughly translates as 'bold speech'. The person who makes such a bold statement is called a *parrhesiastes*. Two qualities are necessary for a proposition to count as parrhesia. One is that the speaker incurs some personal risk from various social or political forces. The second is that the speaker's words must be true. (Thus, a person who creates controversy for the sake of creating controversy is not a parrhesiates.) Today we might call such people **'whistle-blowers'**: individuals who act like referees in a game who stops some player who breaks the rules. Whistle-blowers are people who draw public attention to some act or policy of moral wrongdoing in their workplaces, their governments, or in any other social group to which they belong. Whistleblowers often face all kinds of problems: harassment, defamation of their reputations, job losses, lawsuits, vandalism of their homes and vehicles, and in some cases death threats. But no public cause has ever succeeded "by itself", without courageous people willing to speak out in favour of it. To be a courageous thinker means to care more for the truth than for one's personal interests (and sometimes, more than for one's safety). But it also means to be an agent for necessary changes.

2.2.5 Healthy Skepticism

Earlier, we characterized 'excessive skepticism' as a bad habit. But there is another side of skepticism that is very healthy. Healthy skepticism is **the general unwillingness to accept that things are always what they appear to be.** It is the unwillingness to take things for granted, or to accept that things are as you have been told they are by anyone else, no matter who they are, or what their relation is to you.

This does not mean we have to doubt absolutely everything, nor does it mean we cannot trust anyone. It does, however, mean that we do not jump to conclusions. Healthy skepticism is to be slow to accept the popular explanations for things. It prefers to investigate many possibilities before settling on the best available explanation.

Healthy skepticism is also known as 'reasonable doubt'. We'll see more of that in a later chapter.

2.2.6. Autonomy

To think with autonomy simply means to think for yourself, and not to let other people do your thinking for you. Autonomous thinking is thinking that does not blindly accept what you have been told by parents, friends, role models of every kind, governments, newspaper columnists, or anyone who could have an influence on your thinking.

No one else can do your thinking for you. And

41

you are under no obligation to follow anybody's party line. Your only obligation for thinking, if it is an 'obligation' at all, is to think clearly, consistently, rationally, and (where necessary) courageously.

At the end of some curious, courageous, and skeptical soul-searching, you might decide that your world view should be more or less the same as that which is held by your family, friends, role models, and other influences. That is okay – the point is that the world view is now yours, and not handed to you by others.

42

2.2.7 Simplicity

Sometimes you may find that things are more complex or more elaborate than they appear to be at first. And it is often the job of reason to uncover layers of complexity behind appearances. Still, if you have two or more explanations for something, all of which are about as good as each other, the explanation you should prefer is the simplest one.

This principle of simplicity in good reasoning is sometimes called **Ockham's Razor**. It was first articulated by a Franciscan monk named Brother William of Ockham, who lived from 1288 to 1348. His actual words were "Entia non sunt multiplicanda sine necessitate."[8] In English, this means 'No unnecessary repetition of identicals'. This is a fancy way of saying, 'Well it's possible that there are twenty-three absolutely identical tables occupying exactly the same position in space and time, but it's much simpler to believe that there's just one table here. So let's go with the simpler explanation'. Ockham's original point was theological: he wanted to explain why monotheism is better than polytheism. It's simpler to assume there's one infinite God, than it is to assume there are a dozen or more.

Ockham's idea has also been applied to numerous other matters, from devising scientific theories to interpreting poetry, film, and literature. Other ways to express this idea go like this: "All other things being equal, the simplest explanation tends to be the truth"; and "The best explanation is the one which makes the fewest assumptions."

2.2.8 Precision

There are a lot of words in every language that have more than one meaning. This is a good thing: it allows us more flexibility of expression; it is part of what makes poetry possible; and so on. But for the purpose of reasoning as clearly and as systematically as possible, it is important to use our words very carefully. This usually means avoiding metaphors, symbols, rhetorical questions, weasel words, euphemisms, tangents, equivocations, and 'double speak'. When building a case for why something is true, or something else is not true, and so on, it is important to say exactly what one means, and to eliminate ambiguities as much as possible.

The simplest way to do this is to craft good definitions. A definition can be imprecise in several ways; here are some of them.

- *Too broad:* it covers more things than it should.
- *Too narrow:* it covers too few things.
- *Circular:* the word being defined, or one of its closest synonyms, appears in the definition itself.
- *Too vague:* The definition doesn't really say much at all about what is being defined, even though it looks like it does.

Example of a broad definition: "All dogs are four-legged animals." (Does that mean that all four-legged animals are dogs?)

Example of a narrow definition: "All tables are furniture pieces placed in the dining rooms of houses and used for serving meals." (Does that mean that tables in other rooms used for other purposes are not 'true' tables?)

Example of a Circular definition: "Beauty is that which a given individual finds beautiful." (This actually tells us nothing about what beauty is.)

Example of a vague definition: "Yellowism is not art or anti-art. Examples of Yellowism can look like works of art but are not works of art. We believe that the context for works of art is already art."[9] (And I don't know what this means at all.)

---

8 William of Occam, Sentences of Peter Lombard, (ed. Lugd., 1495), i, dist. 27, qu. 2, K.

9 Marcin Lodyga and Vladimir Umanets, "Manifesto of Yellowism", retrieved from www.thisisyellowism.com, 8 July 2010 / 17 February 2012.

2.2.9 Patience

Good philosophical thinking takes time. Progress in good critical thinking is often very slow. The process of critical thinking can't be called successful if it efficiently maximizes its inputs and outputs in the shortest measure of time: we do not produce thoughts in the mind like widgets in a factory.

The reason for this is because good critical thinking often needs to uncover that which subtle, hard to discern at first, and easy to overlook. I define subtlety as 'a small difference or a delicate detail which takes on greater importance the more it is contemplated.' As a demonstration, think of how many ways you can utter the word 'Yes', and mean something different every time. This also underlines the importance of precision, as a good thinking habit. As another example: think of how the colour planes in a painting by Piet Mondrian, such as his 'Composition with Yellow, Blue, and Red' have squares of white framed by black lines, but none of the white squares are exactly the same shade of white. You won't notice this if you look at the painting for only a few seconds, or if you view a photo of the painting on your computer screen, and your monitor's resolution isn't precise enough to render the subtle differences. But it is the job of reason to uncover those subtleties and lay them out to be examined directly. And the search for those subtleties cannot be rushed.

2.2.10 Consistency

When we looked at what a world view is, we defined it as 'the sum of a set of related answers to the most important questions in life'. It's important that one's world view be consistent: that your answers to the big questions generally cohere well together, and do not obviously contradict each other. Inconsistent thinking usually leads to mistakes, and can produce the uncomfortable feeling of cognitive dissonance. And it can be embarrassing, too. If you are more consistent, you might still make mistakes in your thinking. But it will be a lot easier for you to identify those mistakes, and fix them.

Consistency also means staying on topic, sticking

to the facts, and following an argument to its conclusion. Obviously it can be fun to explore ideas in a random, wandering fashion. But as one's problems grow more serious, it becomes more important to stay the course. Moreover, digressing too far from the topic can also lead you to commit logical fallacies such as Straw Man, and Red Herring.

2.2.11 Open-ness and open-mindedness

Being open-minded means listening to others, taking their views seriously, and treating their ideas with respect even while critically examining them (a difficult thing to do, but not impossible). It also means not resorting to fear and force when promoting one's own views, but rather presenting them in a way that leaves them open to the critical scrutiny of others. In philosophy this is sometimes called **"the principle of charity".** The Principle of Charity requires speakers and listeners to interpret and understand each other's ideas in the very best possible light. Listeners must assume that other speakers are rational (unless you have good reasons to assume otherwise), and that what they say is rational, even if that rationality is not immediately obvious. Philosophers do this partially as a kind of professional courtesy to each other. Open-ness and open-mindedness does not, however, mean that we have to accept everyone's ideas as equally valid. Open mindedness is not the same as assuming that all things are true; it is also not the same as relativism. Rather, the open-minded person looks for the best explanation for things, whether he or she personally likes that explanation or not, and whether it fits with his or her world view or not. She is open to the idea that she might be wrong about something, or that her world view might be partially faulty, or that her thinking about something that matters to her may have to change. But she does not change her thinking at random: she is interested in the truth, whatever it might be.

An open-minded person may still find that some ideas, arguments, and explanations are better than others. But if we are open-minded, then we can be more confident that we have understood other people's views properly: we will not fall into the logical trap of the straw man (see the chapter on Fallacies). It is also much easier to find common ground with others, which is an essential step in quelling conflict. And if we reject some idea, we will have rejected it for the right reasons. Open-mindedness also helps prevent intellectual or ideological differences from descending into personal grudges.

Open-mindedness is also helpful in other ways. Suppose that some friends of mine and I went on a picnic in the park, but soon after we got to our picnic site it started to rain. One member of the party might say the rain was caused by ghosts or supernatural creatures who live in the park and who don't want us to picnic there. Another might say that the rain was caused by air pressure changes in the upper atmosphere. Now the open-minded person is not necessarily the one who accepts that both explanations are equally possible, and leaves it at that. The open- minded person is the one who goes looking for the evidence for each explanation. If he doesn't find the evidence for one of those explanations, he rejects it and goes in search of the evidence for another one. The closed-minded person, by contrast, is the one who picks the explanation he likes best, whether or not there's any evidence for it, and then refuses to consider any alternative explanation. Closed-mindedness is one of the signs that someone's mind is occupied by a value program. As a rule of thumb, the closed-minded person is usually the one who is quickest to accuse other people of being closed-minded, especially when his own ideas are criticized.

The point of that example is to show how open-mindedness helps people arrive at good explanations for things that happen. It does not mean that all explanations for things are equally 'valid'. We do not have to put unlikely or weird explanations on the same footing as those with verifiable evidence or a consistent logical structure. But it can mean that every explanation or idea which appears to be sound, at least at first glance, is given a fair examination, no matter where that explanation came from, or who thought of it first.

2.2.12 Asking for help

So far, I have been stressing good thinking habits that one can practice on one's own. Good thinking tends to require independence and autonomy. And problems often arise when we allow other people to have too much influence over one's own thinking, such as when we allow ourselves to be influenced by peer pressure. However, it can also be helpful to ask others who you respect and admire, or who you believe may have relevant knowledge, to help you. And while it is important to make your own decisions about your own life, there's nothing wrong with asking others who you trust to offer you advice and guidance. And even if you do not ask anyone to offer suggestions, it can sometimes be helpful to hear a different point of view, or just to talk things over with someone who can be both critical and appreciative. The shared wisdom and experience of one's friends, elders, and associates can often lead to different perspectives and better decisions. Others people, for instance, can offer possibilities that you might not have thought of. Or they might know things that you didn't know, and thus point you in new directions. Or they might have faced a similar problem or situation in the past, and their description of their experience might help clarify something about your own situation. As an example, here's the Roman philosopher Seneca describing how some kind of social interaction is important for one's personal intellectual growth: "Skilled wrestlers are kept up to the mark by practice; a musician is stirred to action by one of equal proficiency. The wise man also needs to have his virtues kept in action; and as he prompts himself to do things, so he is prompted by another wise man." [10]

A lot may depend on who you choose to ask for advice, how much you trust them, and how often you go to them. But the overall point here is that knotty and complicated problems need not always be handled alone. A habit of asking one's elders, peers, colleagues, and friends for help can often help clarify one's thinking, and lead to better solutions.

10 Seneca, Letters to Lucilius, 109, 2; trans. R. M. Grummere: Loeb Classical Library

2.3 A few summary remarks for Chapter Two

None of the bad habits of thinking *necessarily* or *inevitably* lead to unsound arguments, false beliefs, or faulty world views. They are not the same as *fallacies* (to be discussed in chapter 5.) An argument can be strong and sound even if its conclusion coincides with the speaker's personal interests, or even if it coincides with the presuppositions of the speaker's culture, etc. The bad habits are, however, **signs that one's thinking is probably not fully clear, critical, and rational**. It may even mean that one has given up the search for the truth of the matter too soon.

Similarly, the good habits, by themselves, do not guarantee that one's thinking will always be perfectly rational, but they do make one's thinking *very much more likely* to be rational.

2.4 Exercises for Chapter Two.

Consider the following situations, and ask yourself which of the good thinking habits should be applied here, and what might happen if some of the bad habits are applied instead.

- You come home at the end of the day and someone sitting on the ground near your door appears to be crying. Perhaps he is injured, or emotionally distraught. Other people passing by seem to be taking no notice, and may even be crossing the street to avoid him.
- Someone who you are fairly close to, such as a member of your family, or a colleague at your workplace, or someone you count as a good friend, unexpectedly utters a nasty racist or sexist or politically prejudiced joke. By his tone of voice and body language, you can tell that he expects you to agree with him or to go along with it.
- Someone you are fairly close to tells you that he has just been diagnosed with a medical condition that carries a strong social stigma, such as cancer, or AIDS. Or, he says he is coming "out of the closet" about his sexual preferences, or that he is changing his religion. He tells you that most of his other friends have stopped associating with him because of this situation.
- Someone who you counted on to do something for you,

for instance someone with whom you have a contract, fails to uphold his promises. This person has failed you numerous times before, but you're fairly sure that confronting this person might have bad consequences for you. For instance, it might result in a lost friendship, or a malicious gossip campaign against you, a loss of money spent on the arrangement, etc.

- A friend of yours at your school, your workplace, or a social club you belong to, has been accused of a crime. The police haven't been called because all the evidence against that person is circumstantial, and it's mostly a matter of one person's word against another's. But around half of your friends are gossiping about that person as if he's obviously guilty, and the other half of your friends are certain he's innocent.
- Have you ever been in a similar situation? What were your thoughts about it? And what did you do?

45

Every S is P   No S is P

A   contraries   E

subalterns   subcontraries·subcontraries   subalterns

I   subcontraries   O

Some S is P   Some S is not P

Chapter Three: Basics of Argumentation

Let's define argumentation as the process of seriously debating the worth and the merits of some proposition. The word 'argument' here does not refer to an angry shouting match. Rather, it refers to **any two (or more) statements in which one is the reason for the other**; one is supported by the other(s), or one follows from the other(s). We 'build' arguments by assembling together basic statements into particular structures, and having assembled them together that way, we can more easily test to see whether the ideas being discussed are worth your time.

3.1. Propositions

Arguments have various parts. And the part that's easiest to identify is called the **proposition**: also sometimes called the **statement**, or the **claim**. (For the purpose of understanding argumentation, these terms mean the same thing, and are often used interchangeably.) A proposition is **a simple sentence that has just one meaning**, for it expresses one thought according to the rules of grammar in one's language. Also, a proposition **asserts that something is the case, or is not the case.** When a proposition asserts that something *is* the case, it is also called an **affirmation**; when a proposition asserts that something *is not* the case, it is also called a **negation** or **denial**.

Not all sentences are propositions. Some sentences are questions, some are commands, some are emotional exclamations, and some are poetic devices like metaphors. One way to recognize a statement is to look for sentences that could be given as a direct

answer to a straightforward question. Another is to look for sentences that could be either true or false; a sentence that one could agree with, or disagree with.

With that in mind, which of the following sentences are propositions?

- The lamp on my table is switched on.
- Good morning everyone!
- My sweater is green.
- How many cars are parked outside right now?
- Smoking is bad for your health.
- Smoking is good for your health.
- Stop driving on the wrong side of the road.
- The revolution will not be televised.
- My love is like a red, red rose.
- WTF?

Also, it is possible for a single sentence to contain within it more than one proposition.

- It's raining today, and I'm feeling blue. (Two propositions)
- The book on my table is well-read, but boring. (Two propositions.)
- This new kitchen gadget can slice any vegetable, as well as any fruit, but it can't handle meat. (Three propositions.)

And, it's also possible to have a paragraph of dialogue in which only one or two sentences are propositions, and the rest of the paragraph is made of expressions that, while they might help communicate the speaker's feelings, are not expressions that can be used to build an argument. Consider this example:

> "The other day, I was really pissed off. I ordered this new computer from the Internet. And it took three weeks to get here, which was bad enough. Then when it arrived I got so mad again! Because the one I ordered was silver, but the one they sent me was black! Somebody in that company is asleep at the wheel."

Clearly, the speaker here is angry about this situation. But if the speaker wanted to draw any logical conclusions from this discussion, for instance about what to do, or about whether to trust the company again, the only relevant sentences here are the ones which stick to the facts. Here's the same discussion again, with the irrelevant expressions crossed out:

> "~~The other day, I was really pissed off~~. I ordered this new computer from the Internet. And it took three weeks to get here, ~~which was bad enough. Then when it arrived I got so mad again! Because~~ the one I ordered was silver, but the one they sent me was black! ~~Somebody in that company is really asleep at the wheel.~~"

As you can see (I hope!), it's really easy to tell the difference between a sentence that is a decent and useful proposition, and another that isn't. Logic starts to look complicated when there are lots of propositions with lots of relations to each other. But even the argument with thousands of lines is still made of simple, straightforward true-or-false sentences like these. The other parts of the argument have to do with the way that propositions are used, or the way they are positioned in relation to other propositions in the general structure of the argument. If you can figure out this part of the textbook, you can figure out everything else!

Once we have sorted out which sentences are propositions and which sentences are not, we are almost ready to put them together into arguments. It's possible to have a sentence which is a proposition, but which you can't use in an argument because of vagueness or an ambiguity in its words or grammar.

For example:

> "Women are stronger than men."

This looks like a perfectly ordinary proposition: it could be either true or false. We could stage arm-wrestling or weight lifting competitions to test it. But is that what the word 'stronger' means here? Or, does it mean that women have more willpower than men? Does it mean that women have thicker and tougher bones than men? Does this statement generalize about the 'average man' or the 'average woman'? If we do not have the context or the meaning of the word 'stronger' here, then this proposition is probably too vague to be used in an argument. The various uses of the word "stronger" are homonyms, and the sentence is vague because we don't know which sense it is that the speaker or writer means. That is an issue separate from the issue of whether the proposition, once properly understood, is true or false.

> "People who get good marks in school are very intelligent."

Again, this looks like a decent proposition, but one might want to clarify the meaning of the word 'intelligent' before using it in an argument. The problem here isn't just that someone could counter-propose that some intelligent people get bad marks in school, or that some stupid people get good marks. Those kinds of issues can come up when the argumentation is underway. But before we get that far, we have to know what the speaker means by the word 'intelligent'. Is it just a matter of the ability to perform well on school tests? Is it the ability to speak clearly and sound like you know what you're talking about? Is it the ability to solve problems quickly? Is it something else?

> "Beer is better than wine."

A judgment of value can act as a decent proposition. But in an example like this one, we would need to know what measure of value is being used here. Is beer considered better because it is cheaper? Or because

48

it has less alcohol content? Or because it's easier for people to make their own beer at home? Or, is this person merely expressing a personal taste preference? Also, given that there are thousands of recipes for beer, and thousands of recipes for wine, it might not be clear what kind of beer and what kind of wine is being compared.

It is often the case that propositions like these are clarified by introducing the argument with a few handy definitions. The definitions might not form part of the argument, but they can provide the context or the background information that will allow debaters to understand each other and then decide whether they agree or disagree.

Propositions can also be clarified by their position in the argument, and their relationship to other propositions.

3.2 Parts of Arguments

Once we have figured out what a proposition is we can build arguments by arranging propositions into particular relationships with other propositions. Remember, an argument needs at least two propositions, not just one.

The first type of proposition that an argument needs is a **premise**. This is a statement given in support of another statement; it is the *reason* why another statement should be accepted as true. Propositions can come from your world view, or your personal experience, or some other trustworthy source. Most arguments have more than one premise and most arguments state the premises first.

The other type of proposition that an argument needs is a **conclusion**. This is the 'point' of an argument; it is that which is supported by the premises; it is that which the speaker is trying to persuade another person to believe is the case. Rather than coming from your experience or your world view or some other source, the conclusion follows from the premises of the argument.

The difference between the premises of an argument and its conclusion are not differences in the statements themselves. Rather, to identify which are the premises and which is the conclusion, you have to rely on context. What is being used as a reason, and what is supposed to follow from those reasons? Sometimes a conclusion that follows from a number of premises is then used as a premise for another conclusion. Consider the following argument:

> "I don't believe he's telling the truth. You see how his eyebrow twitches, and he's sweating a little more than normal. If he is lying, you shouldn't give him your money."

In this example there are two arguments. The speaker intends to support the conclusion that "he is not telling the truth/he is lying" with the premises that "his eyebrow twitches" and "he's sweating more than normal". The conclusion that "he is lying" is used again as a premise, to support the conclusion that "you shouldn't give him your money", which is the *overall conclusion* of the argument.

Stories, poems, explanations, speeches, and so on, can sometimes look like arguments. They might even be made up of statements. But if they do not have premises giving you reasons for accepting conclusions, then they are not arguments. This, in case I haven't mentioned it yet, is why thinking logically about something is often called 'reasoning' about it.

The other parts of arguments have to do with the way premises and conclusions are put together.

An **inference** is the name for the relationship between statements in an argument. It is a line of logic between propositions that lead you from the premises to the conclusion. Inferences are often embodied in certain **indicator words**, which show you which way the direction of the argument is flowing. Here are a few examples of indicator words:

- Because
- Since
- Given that...
- Which means that...
- We can conclude that...
- Hence
- It follows that...

- Therefore
- Consequently…
- This implies…

…and so on. I've mentioned that an argument needs at least two propositions. But two propositions placed side by side do not make an argument. There must be a relationship between them, showing that one leads you to the other, one supports the other, and one follows from the other. That relationship is called an inference; and between its propositions an argument must have inferences too, or else it is not an argument. The indicator words "Because", "Since", "Given that" (and many others) indicate that what follows the indicator word is being used as a premise or reason to support a conclusion. Indicator words that indicate the conclusion are "Which means that", "We can conclude that", "Hence", "Therefore", "Consequently", etc.

3.3 Truth and Validity

Truth, in this way of understanding logic, is a property of propositions. As we've already seen, arguments must be made of sentences that could be either true or false, and not from other kinds of sentences. And there are various ways we could find out whether a given proposition is true. For example:

- The proposition corresponds to the facts, as you are able to observe them or somehow prove them (this is called the **Correspondence** theory of truth).
- The proposition is acceptably consistent, or 'coheres well', with other statements that form part of your world view (the **Coherence** theory).
- When put to some kind of test, the proposition turns out to be a very useful and practical thing to believe (the **Pragmatic** theory).

As truth is a property of sentences, so **validity** is a property of inferences. We say that an argument is valid if its inferences lead you properly from premises to conclusions. Validity is determined by looking at the form, or the structure of the argument, and *not* the content – those are two separate issues.

And finally, **soundness** is a property of arguments as a whole. An argument is sound if it has true premises and valid inferences. Both of these conditions must be met

Arguments themselves also come in two main types: **deduction** and induction. A deduction, or a deductive argument, is a type of argument that, if it begins with true premises, logically guarantees that the conclusion is also true. Deduction works because in a deductive argument, nothing appears in the conclusion that was not already present in at least one of the premises. You can think of a deductive argument as a kind of 'unpacking' or 'synthesizing' of the premises.

An **induction**, or an inductive argument, is a type of argument that asserts the likelihood of the conclusion. In an inductive argument, if the premises are true, then the conclusion is probably true. Unlike a deduction, an induction can go beyond what is asserted in the premises. Its conclusion can say more than what the premises say. For example, you can use an induction to make a prediction about the future. But an induction cannot guarantee the truth of a conclusion, as a deduction can do.

3.4 Types of Statements (Modern Logic)

As we said earlier, an argument is a set of statements from which we can infer another statement, that is, the argument's conclusion. In formal logic there are several common forms of statements that will be useful to know when we discuss argument forms.

3.4.1. Negative Statements

A negative statement is true when the corresponding positive statement is false. For instance, if we were to take the positive statement, "I can clone this pig", the negation of that statement could be expressed by any of the following examples:

- I can not clone this pig.
- It is not the case that I can clone this pig.
- It is false that I can clone this pig.
- It is untrue that I can clone this pig.

If we symbolize "I can clone this pig" with the letter "A", and its negation as "~A", then we can represent the truth values for "A" and "~A" in a table. Row one of this table says that if A is true, then ~A is false. Row two of the table says that if A is false, ~A is true.

A	~A
T	F
F	T

3.4.2 Conjunctions

When a statement affirms or denies more than one thing, that statement is a **conjunction**. In essence, a conjunction claims that all of the statements of which it is composed are true. The individual statements of a conjunction are its **conjuncts**. These statements could be negative or positive. But when any one of the statements of which a conjunction is composed is false, the whole conjunction is false. For instance, the conjunction "My house is red, and I like to eat buttons," is only true if both of the individual statements are true; that is, if my house is red *and* I like to eat buttons. If I don't like to eat buttons, then the conjunction, "My house is red, and I like to eat buttons" is false. But conjunctions don't necessarily use the word "and", and so it is useful to recognize some other indicator words that tell us we're dealing with a conjunction. Consider the following examples, all of which could be reduced to the conjunction, "I childproofed the house, and children get in the house":

- I've childproofed the house, *and* they still get in.
- I've childproofed the house, *but* they still get in.
- I've childproofed the house, *yet* they still get in.
- *Although* I've childproofed the house, they still get in.
- *Even though* I've childproofed the house, they still get in.
- I've childproofed the house; *however*, they still get in.

If we symbolize "I've childproofed the house" as "A" and "Children get in the house" as "B", and the conjunction as "A&B", then the truth table for the conjunction is as follows:

A	B	**A&B**
T	T	**T**
T	F	**F**
F	T	**F**
F	F	**F**

From this we can see that the only case where the conjunction "A&B" is true is when both of the individual statements are true.

Conjunctions are used when we need to put two or more statements together and treat them all as if they are one single statement. This can make it easier to analyze an argument as a whole.

3.4.3 Disjunctions

Disjunctions, like conjunctions, are composed of two or more statements, which could be positive or negative. It is another way to put two statements together and treat them as if they are one statement; but we do this when we know only one of them is true, but we are not sure which one. The statements disjoined in a disjunction are called its **disjuncts**. In the case of disjunctions, only one of those statements needs to be true to make the disjunction as a whole true. For instance, the statement, "Either I'll save this money, or I'll spend it on candy" is true in either of the cases where I save the money or spend it on candy. The statement would be false, however, if instead I bought a motorcycle with the money. All of the following examples are cases of a disjunction:

- The hoarder will clean the house, *or* be evicted.
- *Either* the hoarder will clean the house, or he'll be evicted.
- The hoarder will either clean *or* be evicted.
- *Unless* the hoarder cleans the house, he will be evicted.

If we symbolize "The hoarder will clean the house" as "A", and "The hoarder will be evicted" as "B", then the disjunction as a whole would be represented as "A∨B". We can summarize the truth of the disjunction in a table. From this we can see that a disjunction is true

51

in all of the cases where A is true, B is true, and where both A and B are true. The only case where the disjunction is false is if both of the statements are false.

A	B	A∨B
T	T	T
T	F	T
F	T	T
F	F	F

52

3.4.4 Conditional Statements

Conditional statements are intended to express a one-way relation between the statements of which it is composed, such that the truth of one implies the truth of the other. In general, a conditional statement takes the form, "If P, then Q". For instance, a conditional statement "If Stacey is going to the party, then I'm not going" implies that my decision about whether to go to the party is dependent on whether Stacey is going (because I hate Stacey).

When we have a conditional statement composed of two statements, we call one the antecedent, and the other the consequent. In the statement, "If P, then, Q", "P" is the antecedent (what goes before), and "Q" is the consequent (what follows).

Conditional statements can also be used to express sufficient and necessary conditions. A sufficient condition is something that is *enough* to bring about an expected result, for instance, "If I get 85% of the questions right, then I will get an A on the exam." A necessary condition is something that might not be enough, but is necessary, for instance "If I'm going to write the exam at all, then I'll need to bring a pencil."

Conditional statements can be symbolized with an arrow telling us which way the relation goes. For instance, if "P" symbolizes "You will give me that pony" and "C" symbolizes, "I will cry", all of the following statements would be symbolized "~P→C". Note that "~P" is the negation of "P".

- *If* you don't give me that pony, *then* I'll cry.
- *If* you don't give me that pony, I'll cry.
- I'll cry *only if* you don't give me that pony.

- Your not giving me that pony *is a sufficient condition* to make me cry.
- My crying is *necessary*, given that I haven't gotten my pony.
- *Unless* you give me that pony, I'll cry.
- *When* I don't get my pony, I cry.
- I cry *only when* I don't get my pony.

A conditional statement is true if both of the statements of which it is composed are true, or if the consequent is true. It is only false if the antecedent is true and the consequent is false. This is the only case where we can be sure that the relationship does not hold. For instance, if Stacey goes to the party and I go too, then the statement "If Stacey is going to the party, then I'm not going" is false, because in fact we have shown that my hatred of Stacey is not strong enough to prevent me from having a good time. However, if I don't go to the party, it might be because Stacey is going, or it might be for another reason. Thus in any case where I don't go to the party, we say that the conditional statement is true.

The truth of the conditional statement A→B can be summarized in the following table:

A	B	A→B
T	T	T
T	F	F
F	T	T
F	F	T

3.4.5 Biconditional Statements

A biconditional statement describes a two-way relationship between two statements, such that either one implies the other. For instance, if my decision to go to the party depends on my being able to bring my cat, and if I don't get to bring my cat, then I won't go, then there are two possible results: Either I get to bring my cat, and so I go to the party, or they won't let me bring my cat, so I won't go. This means that the two-way relation holds if the truth of the statements is the same. Either both are true, or both are false.

All of the following statements describe a biconditional relation, for the case in which if you eat your vegetables you will get dessert, and if you don't eat your vegetables, you won't.

- You can have dessert *if and only if* you eat your vegetables.
- You can have dessert *exactly if* you eat your vegetables.
- You can have dessert *precisely* if you eat your vegetables.
- Your eating your vegetables is a *necessary* and *sufficient condition* for your getting dessert.
- You can have your dessert, *if* you eat your vegetables, *but only if* you eat them.
- You can have your dessert *just in case* you eat your vegetables.

We can summarize the truth of a biconditional statement in a table:

A	B	**A↔B**
T	T	**T**
T	F	**F**
F	T	**F**
F	F	**T**

3.5 Categorical Logic

Categorical logic is a type of deductive logic introduced by Aristotle in the 4th century BC, according to which we can infer true statements from other true statements that state that some or all things of a category belong to another category. For instance, the statement that "All cats are blue" tells us that there is a category of cats, and a category of blue things, and that everything that is a cat is also blue. In categorical logic, we can divide a statement into parts, each part describing a category. This is something we cannot do if we are only evaluating statements as a whole. For instance, if I claim that "All cats are blue" and that "Benny is a cat", then the logical inference we can make is that "Benny is blue". But if we're looking at the propositions as a whole, then we can't see the relation between the two statements. That is, if we symbolized "All cats are blue" as "A", and "Benny is a cat" as "B", then we have lost

the relation between the two claims that allows us to infer that "Benny is blue".

There are four main types of categorical statements. We will use "S" to indicate the subject of the proposition, and "P" to indicate the predicate we are attributing to the subject.

Universal Affirmative: All S are P.
Example: "All cats are fuzzy." (S: cats. P: fuzzy things.)

Universal Negative: No S are P
Example: "No dogs are ten feet tall." (S: dogs. P: things that are ten feet tall.)

Particular Affirmative: Some S are P
Example: "Some skyscrapers are beautiful." (S: skyscrapers. P: beautiful things.)

Particular Negative: Some S are not P
Example: "Some books are not meant for children." (S: books. P: things meant for children.)

Modern logic has a similar "predicate logic", which extends beyond the realm of this text. In fact, attempts to symbolize Aristotle's logic have resulted in horrible difficulties and frustrated logicians all over the world for millennia. One particular difference between Aristotle's logic and modern predicate logic we should note is that while modern logic would symbolize Aristotle's universal statements as conditional statements, Aristotle did not use conditionals in his logic, as he believed a conditional statement did not properly express the relation between the antecedent and the consequent. The proper relation is that of belonging to a category. This is why you might see "All S are P" reinterpreted by modern logicians as something like, "If X is an S, then X is a P" (where X is some random individual). Modern logic also assumes that when we make a statement about a particular thing, that particular thing exists, but when we make a universal statement, the subject of that statement doesn't necessarily exist. Thus particular statements are said to have "existential import" that universal statements do not.

Contradictories

In Categorical Logic, two statements are said to be contradictories if it is impossible for both of them to be true, and also impossible that both of them should be false. For instance, "I'm wearing white shoes" and "I'm not wearing white shoes" are contradictory statements.

Of the kinds of statements given above, the Universal Affirmative is contradictory to the Particular Negative, and the Universal Negative is contradictory to the Particular Affirmative. This is best illustrated by example. Let's say that "S" stands for "cats" and "P" stands for "fuzzy". Then the statements look like this:

- Universal Affirmative: All cats are fuzzy
- Universal Negative: No cats are fuzzy
- Particular Affirmative: Some cat is fuzzy
- Particular Negative: Some cat is not fuzzy

The Universal Affirmative and Particular Negative statements are contradictory because *it is impossible* that all cats are fuzzy and that at the same time some cat is not fuzzy. It is also impossible that both statements are false. That would mean that "All cats are not fuzzy" and "Some cat is fuzzy" would both have to be true.

Likewise, the Universal Negative and the Particular Affirmative statements are contradictory. Again, this is because *it is impossible* that "No cats are fuzzy" and "Some cat is fuzzy" are both true statements. Likewise, they cannot both be false. This would mean that "No cat is not fuzzy" and "Some cat is not fuzzy" would both have to be true.

Contraries

Two statements are said to be *contraries* if it is impossible for them both to be true, but possible for them both to be false. Carrying on with our fuzzy cats, the Universal Affirmative and Universal Negative statements are contraries. "All cats are fuzzy" and "No cats are fuzzy" cannot be true at the same time. However, they could both be false. When they are both false is when both of their contradictory statements are true: when some cats are fuzzy and some are not.

Subcontraries

Two statements are said to be *subcontraries* if it is possible for them both to be true, but impossible for them both to be false. The Particular Affirmative and Particular Negative statements are subcontraries, as it is possible for "Some cats are fuzzy" and "Some cats are not fuzzy" to be true at the same time. But both statements cannot be false at the same time. Then both of their contradictories would have to be true: "All cats are fuzzy" and "No cats are fuzzy". (But this is impossible.)

Subalterns

Since categorical logic did not distinguish between statements having existential import and those that did not, it is also possible to make inferences from Universal Statements to Particular Statements. That is, categorical logic assumes that if "All cats are fuzzy" then "Some cat is fuzzy". Similarly, if "No cats are fuzzy", then "Some cat is not fuzzy".

The Square of Opposition

The above conclusions can be (and often are) summarized in a diagram[11]:

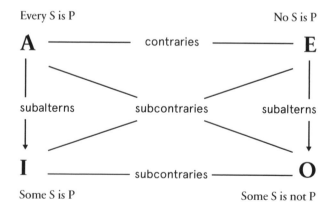

Every S is P   No S is P

A ——————— contraries ——————— E

subalterns   subcontraries   subalterns

I ——————— subcontraries ——————— O

Some S is P   Some S is not P

3.6 Some Common Deductive Argument Forms

Earlier we stated that the definition of an argument is **"any two (or more) statements in which one is the reason for the other".** This section will introduce some valid deductive argument forms. In deductive

11 Diagram taken from Parsons, Terence, "The Traditional Square of Opposition", The Stanford Encyclopedia of Philosophy (Fall 2012 Edition), Edward N. Zalta (ed.), URL = http://plato.stanford.edu/archives/fall2012/entries/square/

argumentation, we take some number of premises as given, and from these we are able to make other claims according to certain logical rules of inference. If the conclusion that results comes out of the given premises as a result of applying the accepted rules of inference, then we say that the conclusion follows necessarily from the premises, or that the argument is "valid".

The validity of an argument is determined not by what it says, but by its *form*. That means that when we assess the validity of an argument, we assume that the premises are true. If, on the other hand, we want to question the truth of the premises, we would be evaluating not its validity, but its *soundness*. Consider the following argument:

> All pigs can fly.
> Babe is a pig.
> Therefore, Babe can fly.

This argument is valid. That is, assuming that the premises are true, the conclusion necessarily follows. Of course, we can question the *soundness* of the argument. If we can disprove the premise that "All pigs can fly", then the argument would be unsound. We might also question whether we want to consider Babe a pig, rather than a fictional character resembling a pig. In either case, if either one of the premises is not true, then the argument is not sound. But that does not mean it is not valid. An argument can be valid without being sound. Let's look at an example of the same *form*:

> All humans are mortal.
> Brendan is a human.
> Therefore, Brendan is mortal.

This argument is both valid and sound. In fact, both arguments are examples of a categorical syllogism of the form AII (Modus Darii), which is a shorthand for Universal Affirmative-Particular Affirmative-Particular Affirmative. But we'll get to that.

3.6.1 Modus Ponens or Affirming the Antecedent

Modus Ponens is a valid argument form taking a conditional statement as one premise, and the affirmation of its antecedent as another premise. So, if I claim "If something, then another thing" and then affirm "something", I can logically deduce that "another thing". If the conditional statement and the affirmation of its antecedent are both true, the truth of the conclusion is guaranteed.

Let's take an example.

(P1) If the dog is barking, then there's an intruder in the house.
(P2) The dog is barking!
(C) Therefore, there's an intruder in the house!

Of course, there might be other reasons why the dog might bark. But according to Premise 1, the fact that the dog is barking implies that there is definitely an intruder in the house. And we are assuming that P1 is true.

This argument takes the general form:

(P1) If P, then Q
(P2) P
(C) Q

Rendered symbolically:

(P1) $P \rightarrow Q$
(P2) P
(C) Q

The validity of this form is pretty intuitive. But if ever in doubt, we can refer back to our truth table for conditionals and prove it beyond a doubt.

P	Q	$\mathbf{P \rightarrow Q}$
T	T	**T**
T	F	**F**
F	T	**T**
F	F	**T**

Premise 1 gives us a conditional statement. Considered alone, we can see that there are three possible cases where it could be true: where the antecedent (P) is true and the consequent (Q) is true; where the antecedent (P) is false and the consequent (Q) true; and where the antecedent (P) and consequent (Q) are both false. We can therefore eliminate the fourth possibility that the antecedent (P) is true and the consequent (Q) false, because this would make Premise 1 false (and we are assuming that it's true). So let's cross it off.

56

P	Q	P→Q
T	T	T
~~T~~	~~F~~	~~F~~
F	T	T
F	F	T

Now, taking into account Premise 2, which tells us that our antecedent is true, we can eliminate the possibilities in the table where P is false.

P	Q	P→Q
T	T	T
~~T~~	~~F~~	~~F~~
~~F~~	~~T~~	~~T~~
~~F~~	~~F~~	~~T~~

So it seems that the truth of the consequent is guaranteed, for based on what we know from Premise 1 and Premise 2, there is no other possible conclusion.

Let's look at another example:

(P1) If it is raining, then I will need my umbrella.
(P2) It is raining.
(C) Therefore, I will need my umbrella.

There might be other reasons why you might need your umbrella. Perhaps it's to be used as a prop in a theatrical performance. But nothing in this argument tells you that. And besides, whether or not that's the case, the first premise still tells you that you need it when it rains.

Affirming the Consequent: Modus Ponens' Invalid Half Brother
There's a sneaky invalid argument out there that looks a lot like Modus Ponens. What would happen if instead we affirmed the consequent, instead of the antecedent? We would have an argument like this:

(P1) If it is raining, then I will need my umbrella.
(P2) I will need my umbrella.
(P3) Therefore, it is raining.

We tend to make this logical leap and equate the fact that we need our umbrella with the fact that it's raining. But though it is not equally likely that we might need the umbrella for a theatrical performance, it is still a possibility. That is, the fact that I need my umbrella does not *absolutely guarantee* that it's raining. This argument form is therefore invalid.

Practical Uses of Modus Ponens:
Every circuit in your computer uses this pattern of argument to make calculations. In effect, the diodes and transistors in your computer CPU are like 'switches', which operate as if they are reasoning like this:

If a signal comes in from direction X, then send it out again in direction Y.
A signal just came in from direction X.
Therefore, the thing to do is send it out in direction Y.

3.6.2 Modus Tollens or Denying the Consequent

Modus Tollens is a valid argument form taking a conditional statement as one premise, and the denial of its consequent as another premise. So, if I claim "If something, then another thing" and then deny "another thing", I can logically deduce that "not something". Here I'm recognizing that if the relation between "something" and "another thing" holds, and if "another thing" failed to happen, or is false (depending on what that thing is), then "something" must not have happened, or must not be true.

Let's take an example.

(P1) If you gave me a diamond tiara, I'd be the happiest girl in the world!
(P2) I am not the happiest girl in the world.
(C) Therefore, you did not give me a diamond tiara.

This argument takes the general form:

(P1) If P, then Q.
(P2) Not Q.
(C) Not P.

Rendered symbolically:

(P1) P→Q
(P2) ~Q
(C) ~P

Again, the validity of this form is rather intuitive. But, we can still go through the truth table proof, just for fun.

Again, Premise 1 tells us that the conditional statement is true. Therefore, we can again eliminate the possibility that it is false from our table.

P	Q	P→Q
T	T	T
~~T~~	~~F~~	~~F~~
F	T	T
F	F	T

Then, Premise 2 tells us that the consequent (Q) is false. We can therefore also eliminate all of the possibilities where Q is true from our table.

P	Q	P→Q
~~T~~	~~T~~	~~T~~
~~T~~	~~F~~	~~F~~
~~F~~	~~T~~	~~T~~
F	F	T

Now we're left with just what we expect. If P→Q is true, and Q is false, then P must also be false.

Like Modus Ponens's evil half brother, there's another bad argument out there attempting at every turn to pass itself off as valid.

Denying the Antecedent: Fallacy!
Again, when we see a conditional statement and a negation, we're immediately tempted to think 'Modus Tollens'. But what happens if we deny the antecedent instead of the consequent? We get an argument like this:

(P1) If you gave me a diamond tiara, I'd be the happiest girl in the world!
(P2) You did not give me a diamond tiara.
(C) Therefore, I am not the happiest girl in the world.

Again, the truth of these premises does not absolutely guarantee the truth of the conclusion. Even if you did not give me a diamond tiara, I might still be the happiest girl in the world for some other reason. I might have been the happiest girl in the world all along, and there's quite possibly nothing you could do to change that. This argument form is invalid.

3.6.3 Categorical Syllogisms

The four standard statements in categorical logic can be combined into 24 possible valid logical argument forms. But we can just look at a few of them; once you get the idea behind how categorical syllogisms are judged as valid or invalid, it's easy to discern the difference.

One valid categorical syllogism was already given in the introduction to this section. That was:

All humans are mortal.
Brendan is a human.
Therefore, Brendan is mortal.

This argument is valid. We can, in general, conclude that if an entire class of things has some quality, and if something is a member of that class, it has that quality.

But we can also generalize further. If an entire class of things has some quality, and all of the things that have that quality have some other quality, then we can make a valid inference that the entire class also has that other quality.

For example:

> All farm animals are cannibalistic.
> All cows are farm animals.
> Therefore all cows are cannibalistic.

If you accept the validity of the first argument, then you must also accept the validity of this argument. This makes sense, because if every individual cow is a farm animal and therefore cannibalistic, then the whole cow species is cannibalistic.

Now let's try some negative statements.

> No human is immortal.
> Brendan is a human.
> Therefore Brendan is not immortal.

What this argument says is that if none of the members of the class of humans is immortal, then neither is a specific individual of that class. Again, we can generalize. If no specific member of the class is immortal, then the whole class is excluded from immortality.

> No human is immortal.
> All philosophy professors are humans.
> Therefore no philosophy professor is immortal.

These are only some of the possible combinations of categorical statements that result in valid syllogisms. If you can keep track of what thing or what kind of thing belongs to what class, then you're in pretty good shape for evaluating the validity of categorical syllogisms.

3.6.4 Enthymemes

An enthymeme is a categorical syllogism in which one of the premises is missing. People use them all the time, often without realizing it, when they want to get a certain point across quickly, or when they can assume the listeners know what the they are talking about. It's really easy to commit a fallacy called 'undistributed middle' when making an enthymeme, because we aren't always keeping close track of where the premises are. So to analyze an enthymeme, one has to lay out all the propositions in the place where they would stand in a categorical syllogism, fill in the missing proposition, and then determine whether the inferences are valid or invalid.

"Many songs by Justin Timberlake are popular. So this new song will be popular too."
> P1. Some Justin Timberlake songs are popular.
> *P2. This new song is composed by Justin Timberlake.*
> C. Therefore, this new song will be popular.

"He is a leprous man, for he is unclean." (Leviticus 13)
> *P1. Leprous men are unclean.*
> P2. He is unclean.
> C. Therefore, he is a leprous man.

"Yond Cassius has a lean and hungry look. He thinks too much. Such men are dangerous." (Shakespeare, Julius Caesar, III.2)
> P1. Cassius has a lean and hungry look and thinks too much.
> P2. Men who have lean and hungry looks and who think too much are dangerous.
> *C. Therefore, Cassius is dangerous.*

By the way: which of these enthymemes are sound, and which are not?

3.6.5 Hypothetical Syllogism

A hypothetical syllogism is a valid argument form that takes as premises two conditional statements and concludes a third, where the consequent of the first premise is identical to the antecedent of the second.

For instance, if I make the claim,

(P1) If it gets below freezing outside, I can make ice out there.

And I also make the claim that,

(P2) If I can make ice, my soft drinks will be deliciously refreshing.

Then I can conclude that,

(C) If it gets below freezing outside, my soft drinks will be deliciously refreshing.

Essentially, we are demonstrating the transitive property of conditional statements. That is, if we have two conditional statements where the consequent of one is identical to the antecedent of another, we can eliminate them and mash the rest of the two premises together to get a conclusion that is definitely true.

This argument takes the general form

(P1) If P, then Q
(P2) If Q, then R
(C) If P, then R

Rendered symbolically:

(P1) P→Q
(P2) Q→R
(C) P→R

The truth table proof of this argument now has to take into account three terms. Therefore when we make the table, we must account for all of the possible truth values of P, Q, and R, for a total of 8 combinations. Then we can fill in the truth values for the conditional statements acting as our premises:

P	Q	R	P→Q	Q→R
T	T	T	T	T
T	T	F	T	F
T	F	T	F	T
T	F	F	F	T
F	T	T	T	T
F	T	F	T	F
F	F	T	T	T
F	F	F	T	T

If we assume that both P→Q and Q→R are true, we can eliminate all of the possibilities where either one of them is false.

P	Q	R	P→Q	Q→R
T	T	T	T	T
T̶	T̶	F	T̶	F
T̶	F	T̶	F̶	T̶
T̶	F	F	F̶	T̶
F	T	T	T	T
F	T̶	F	T̶	F̶
F	F	T	T	T
F	F	F	T	T

Now let's take the values for P and R that are left over, and see what the values for P→R looks like. There are four possible combinations of P and R left, after we have taken into account the truth of our premises:

P	R	P→R
T	T	T
F	T	T
F	T	T
F	F	T

Now it looks like no matter what leftover values of P and R we might choose, if P→Q and Q→R are true, P→R is definitely going to be true.

But this could all be made clearer by taking a few examples. We can apply the hypothetical syllogism to categorical thinking:

(P1) If Socrates is a man, Socrates is an animal.
(P2) If Socrates is an animal, Socrates is a substance.
(C) If Socrates is a man, Socrates is a substance.

We could also apply the hypothetical syllogism to causal relations:

(P1) If I set the house on fire, it will burn down.
(P2) If the house burns down, I'll collect insurance money.
(C) If I set the house on fire, I'll collect insurance money.

In any case, the transitive property of the implication relation that constitutes a conditional statement guarantees that the hypothetical syllogism is valid. That is, the hypothetical syllogism can be proven valid just by the definition of conditional statements.

3.6.6 Disjunctive Syllogism

This argument establishes the truth of some proposition by ruling out all other possibilities until there's just one left still standing.

60

Form:

> Either P is true, or Q is true.
> P is false.
> Therefore, Q is true.

> Either P is true, or Q is true.
> Q is false.
> Therefore, P is true.

Examples:

> (P1) This tree is either coniferous or it is deciduous.
> (P2) I see by its flat leaves that it is not coniferous.
> (C) Therefore, this tree is deciduous.

> (P1) One of us is going to die here, Mister Bond. It's either you or me.
> (P2) And it isn't going to be me.
> (C) So it will have to be you!

This is a valid argument form:

> (P1) P∨Q
> (P2) ~P
> (C) Q

Truth table proof:
If we take our truth table for disjunction and assume Premise 1 is true, then we have three possible interpretations left: both P and Q are true, P is true and Q is false, or P is false and Q is true:

P	Q	**P∨Q**
T	T	**T**
T	F	**T**
F	T	**T**
F	F	**F**

But Premise 2 tells us that P is false. Therefore we can eliminate some more possibilities and guarantee that Q is true:

P	Q	**P∨Q**
~~T~~	~~T~~	~~T~~
~~T~~	~~F~~	~~T~~
F	T	T
~~F~~	~~F~~	~~F~~

Actually, you can have as many propositions as you like in the first premise, and rule them out one by one in the middle premises until you arrive at the last one standing. So the argument could also look like this:

> Either P, or Q, or R, or S, or T.
> P is false.
> Q is false.
> R is false.
> S is false.
> Therefore, T is true.

This is basically what I mean when I make the argument:

> (P1) You talkin' to me?
> (P2-?) I'm the only one here. (That is, nobody else *is* here—John isn't here, Mary isn't here, Neil isn't here, Bob isn't here, Sheila isn't here—and you must be talking to *someone here.*)
> (C) I guess you're talkin' to me.

Practical Uses:
The game of "Clue" (first published as "Cluedo" in England in 1949) operates entirely on the basis of the disjunctive syllogism. In this game players try to figure out who killed "Mr. Body", by locating suspects, murder

weapons, and crime scenes on a list of possibilities. When a player figures out which suspect, weapon, and location cannot be accounted for, she can make an accusation, and perhaps win the game.

3.6.7 Adjunction

The rule of adjunction allows us to form a conjunction from any two true statements. It is also known as "conjunction introduction". This is one of the most intuitively obvious rules of inference in the world of logic. It simply states that if two statements are true independently, then their conjunction is also true.

For example, from the premises:
(P1) I'm a little man
(P2) I'm also evil
(P3) I'm also into cats

I can conclude:
(C) I'm a little man, and I'm also evil, also into cats.

Generally this is done by adding one premise to another individually, such that a logical proof would look like this:

(P1) P
(P2) Q
(P3) R
(C1) P&Q
(C2) (P&Q)&R

The result is the same.

"Why would we do this?" you might ask. It seems so obvious. Well, there are some cases where you might need a conjunction and don't have one. For instance, say you know that everything that looks like a duck *and* quacks like a duck is a duck, and you want to prove that your mystery pet Billy is a duck. Then we would have an argument like this:

(P1) Everything that looks like a duck and quacks like a duck is a duck.

(P2) Billy looks like a duck.
(P3) Billy quacks like a duck.
(C1) Therefore Billy looks like a duck and quacks like a duck.
(C2) Therefore Billy is a duck.

This rule is valid by the definition of conjunction, whereby we stated that a conjunction is true if and only if all of its conjuncts are true.

3.6.8 Dilemmas

A dilemma, stemming from the Greek "δίλημμα" refers to an "ambiguous proposition". In logic, a dilemma occurs when we have two possibilities somewhere in the argument. Often a dilemma is associated with an undesirable consequence. Consider, for instance, this simple dilemma:

"You're damned if you do, and damned if you don't."

We can separate this dilemma into two conditional statements.

(P1) If you do, then you're damned.
(P2) If you don't, then you're damned.

Then we can take these premises together with the logical truth that either you do or you don't:

(P3) You do or you don't.

And then make the obvious conclusion:

(C) You're damned.

But sometimes our dilemmas are not simple. This section will introduce two complex dilemmas, where our *conclusions* turn out to be ambiguous statements. That is, while we can infer that either *this one or that one* of our possible conclusions is true, we don't know which one. We can, however, confidently state the conclusion that *either this or that.*

61

Constructive Dilemma

The constructive dilemma gives us two conditional statements and a disjunctive statement. For example:

> (P1) If I go to the movies tonight, I'll have to stand in line.
> (P2) If I go to that party tonight, I'll have to do laundry.
> (P3) I'm either going to the movies, or going to the party.

From these statements we can validly conclude:

> (C) I'm either going to have to stand in line, or I'll have to do laundry.

We don't know which one. But one of them is going to happen.

 Notice how similar this argument is to modus ponens. Where in modus ponens we had a conditional statement and a true antecedent, now we have two conditional statements, and another one saying that *one* of the antecedents is going to be true. If we knew which one, we could make a valid modus ponens argument. But we don't. Still, though, we can conclude that depending on my choice of what to do this evening, I'll have to do something unpleasant.

The argument form looks like this:

> (P1) If P, then Q
> (P2) If R, then S
> (P3) P or R
> (C) Q or S

Rendered symbolically:

> (P1) $P \rightarrow Q$
> (P2) $R \rightarrow S$
> (P3) $P \lor R$
> (C) $Q \lor S$

Let's look at another example.

> (P1) If your mother loved you, she would pack you a bagged lunch.
> (P2) If your father loved you, he would knit you some mittens.
> (P3) One of your father or mother loves you.
> Our conclusion is:
> (C) Your mother will pack you a bagged lunch or your father will knit you some mittens.

Note that in this example, it is completely possible that you'll end up with both a bagged lunch and some mittens. This is as a result of the inclusive nature of disjunction. That is, while it is safe to say that either one of your father or mother loves you, it's possible that both do.

Destructive Dilemma

While the constructive dilemma allows us to infer a disjunction using the same kind of reasoning that makes modus ponens valid, a destructive dilemma mirrors closely the same kind of reasoning as modus tollens. In a destructive dilemma, we are again provided with two conditional statements and told that one of their consequents is false. We do not know which one it is, however. The only thing we can say for sure is that if *at least one* of their consequents is false, *at least one* of their antecedents will be as well.

> (P1) If the people value free puppies for all, Jim will win the election.
> (P2) If the people value extended library hours, George will win the election.
> (P3) Either Jim will *not* win the election, or George will *not* win the election.
> (C) Either the people *don't* value free puppies for all, or the people *don't* value extended library hours.

While we might be able to guess at which one of these possibilities is true, neither one of them is assured by the rules of deductive logic. All we know is that *at least one* of the disjuncts in our conclusion will be true.

The argument form looks like this:

(P1) If P, then Q
(P2) If R, then S
(P3) Not Q or Not S
(C) Not P or Not R

Rendered symbolically:

(P1) P→Q
(P2) R→S
(P3) ~Q∨~S
(C) ~P∨~R

Let's take a look at another example.

(P1) If your mother loved you, she would pack you a
bagged lunch.
(P2) If your father loved you, he would knit you
some mittens.
(P3) Since your care package looks rather small, you
infer that it either does not contain a bagged lunch, or it
does not contain mittens.
(C) Either your mother doesn't love you, or your father
doesn't love you.

Again, it's possible that neither of your parents
love you, and that they sent an empty box just to taunt
you. It's cruel, but logically valid.

3.7 Induction

All of the argument forms we have looked at so far
have been deductively valid. That meant, we said, that
the conclusion follows from necessity if the premises
are true. But to what extent can we ever be sure of
the truth of those premises? Inductive argumentation
is a less certain, more realistic, more familiar way of
reasoning that we all do, all the time. Inductive argumentation recognizes, for instance, that a premise like
"All horses have four legs" comes from our previous
experience of horses. If one day we were to encounter
a three-legged horse, deductive logic would tell us that
"All horses have four legs" is false, at which point the

premise becomes rather useless for a deducer. In fact,
deductive logic tells us that if the premise "All horses
have four legs" is false, even if we know there are many,
many four-legged horses in the world, when we go
to the track and see hordes of four-legged horses, all
we can really be certain of is that "There is at least *one*
four-legged horse."

Inductive logic allows for the more realistic
premise, "The vast majority of horses have four legs".
And inductive logic can use this premise to infer other
useful information, like "If I'm going to get Chestnut
booties for Christmas, I should probably get four of
them." The trick is to recognize a certain amount of
uncertainty in the truth of the conclusion, something
for which deductive logic does not allow. In real life,
however, inductive logic is used much more frequently
and (hopefully) with some success. Let's take a look at
some of the uses of inductive reasoning.

Predicting the Future

We constantly use inductive reasoning to predict the
future. We do this by compiling evidence based on
past observations, and by assuming that the future will
resemble the past. For instance, I make the observation
that every other time I have gone to sleep at night,
I have woken up in the morning. There is actually
no certainty that this will happen, but I make the
inference because of the fact that this is what has happened every other time. In fact, it is not the case that
"All people who go to sleep at night wake up in the
morning". But I'm not going to lose any sleep over that.
And we do the same thing when our experience has
been less consistent. For instance, I might make the assumption that, if there's someone at the door, the dog
will bark. But it's not outside the realm of possibility
that the dog is asleep, has gone out for a walk, or has
been persuaded not to bark by a clever intruder with
sedative-laced bacon. I make the assumption that if
there's someone at the door, the dog will bark, because
that is what *usually* happens.

Explaining Common Occurrences

We also use inductive reasoning to explain things that commonly happen. For instance, if I'm about to start an exam and notice that Bill is not here, I might explain this to myself with the reason that Bill is stuck in traffic. I might base this on the reasoning that being stuck in traffic is a common excuse for being late, or because I know that Bill never accounts for traffic when he's estimating how long it will take him to get somewhere. Again, that Bill is actually stuck in traffic is not certain, but I have some good reasons to think it's probable. We use this kind of reasoning to explain past events as well. For instance, if I read somewhere that 1986 was a particularly good year for tomatoes, I assume that 1986 also had some ideal combination of rainfall, sun, and consistently warm temperatures. Although it's possible that a scientific madman circled the globe planting tomatoes wherever he could in 1986, inductive reasoning would tell me that the former, environmental explanation is more likely. (But I could be wrong.)

Generalizing

Often we would like to make general claims, but in fact it would be very difficult to prove any general claim with any certainty. The only way to do so would be to observe every single case of something about which we wanted to make an observation. This would be, in fact, the only way to prove such assertions as, "All swans are white". Without being able to observe every single swan in the universe, I can never make that claim with certainty. Inductive logic, on the other hand, allows us to make the claim, with a certain amount of modesty.

3.7.1 Inductive Generalization

Inductive generalization allows us to make general claims, despite being unable to actually observe every single member of a class in order to make a certainly true general statement. We see this in scientific studies, population surveys, and in our own everyday reason-

ing. Take for example a drug study. Some doctor or other wants to know how many people will go blind if they take a certain amount of some drug for so many years. If they determine that 5% of people in the study go blind, they then assume that 5% of all people who take the drug for that many years will go blind. Likewise, if I survey a random group of people and ask them what their favourite colour is, and 75% of them say "purple", then I assume that purple is the favourite colour of 75% of people. But we have to be careful when we make an inductive generalization. When you tell me that 75% of people really like purple, I'm going to want to know whether you took that survey outside a Justin Bieber concert.

Let's take an example. Let's say I asked a class of 400 students whether or not they think logic is a valuable course, and 90% of them said yes. I can make an inductive argument like this:

(P1) 90% of 400 students believe that logic is a valuable course.
(C) Therefore 90% of students believe that logic is a valuable course.

There are certain things I need to take into account in judging the quality of this argument. For instance, did I ask this in a logic course? Did the respondents have to raise their hands so that the professor could see them, or was the survey taken anonymously? Are there enough students in the course to justify using them as a representative group for students in general?

If I did, in fact, make a class of 400 *logic* students raise their hands in response to the question of whether logic is valuable course, then we can identify a couple of problems with this argument. The first is **bias**. We can assume that anyone enrolled in a logic course is more likely to see it as valuable than any random student. I have therefore skewed the argument in favour of logic courses. I can also question whether the students were answering the question honestly. Perhaps if they are trying to save the professor's feelings, they are more likely to raise their hands and assure her that the logic course is a valuable one.

Now let's say I've avoided those problems. I have assured that the 400 students I have asked are randomly selected, say, by soliciting email responses from randomly selected students from the university's entire student population. Then the argument looks stronger.

Another problem we might have with the argument is whether I have asked *enough* students so that the whole population is well-represented. If the student body as a whole consists of 400 students, my argument is very strong. If the student body numbers in the tens of thousands, I might want to ask a few more before assuming that the opinions of a few mirror those of the many. This would be a problem with my **sample size**.

Let's take another example. Now I'm going to run a scientific study, in which I will pay someone $50 to take a drug with unknown effects and see if it makes them blind. In order to control for other variables, I open the study only to white males between the ages of 18 and 25.

A bad inductive argument would say:
  (P1) 40% of 1000 people who took the drug went blind.
  (C) Therefore 40% of people who take the drug will go blind.

A better inductive argument would make a more modest claim:
  (P1) 40% of the 1000 people who took the drug went blind.
  (C) Therefore 40% of white males between the ages of 18 and 25 who take the drug will go blind.

The point behind this example is to show how inductive reasoning imposes an important limitation on the possible conclusions a study or a survey can make. In order to make good generalizations, we need to ensure that our sample is **representative**, **non-biased**, and **sufficiently sized**.

3.7.2 Statistical Syllogism

Where in an inductive generalization we saw statement expressing a statistic applied to a more general group, we can also use statistics to go from the general to the particular. For instance, if I know that most computer science majors are male, and that some random individual with the androgynous name "Cameron" is an computer science major, then we can be reasonably certain that Cameron is a male. We tend to represent the uncertainty by qualifying the conclusion with the word "probably". If, on the other hand, we wanted to say that something is unlikely, like that Cameron were a female, we could use "probably not". It is also possible to temper our conclusion with other similar qualifying words.

Let's take an example.

  (P1) Of the 133 people found guilty of homicide last year in Canada, 79% were jailed.
  (P2) Socrates was found guilty of homicide last year in Canada.
  (C) Therefore, Socrates was probably jailed.

In this case we can be reasonably sure that Socrates is currently rotting in prison. Now the certainty of our conclusion seems to be dependent on the statistics we're dealing with. There are definitely more certain and more uncertain cases.

  (P1) In the last election, 50% of voting Americans voted for Obama, while 48% voted for Romney.
  (P2) Jim is a voting American.
  (C) Therefore, Jim probably voted for Obama.

Clearly, this argument is not as strong as the first. It is only slightly more likely than not that Jim voted for Obama. In this case we might want to revise our conclusion to say:

  (C) Therefore, it is slightly more likely than not that Jim voted for Obama.

In other cases, the likelihood that something is or is not the case approaches certainty. For example:

  (P1) There is a 0.00000059% chance you will die on any

single flight, assuming you use one of the most poorly rated airlines.

(P2) I'm flying to Paris next week.

(C) There's more than a million to one chance that I will die on my flight.

Note that in all of these examples, nothing is ever stated with absolute certainty. It is possible to improve the chances that our conclusions will be accurate by being more specific, or finding out more information. We would know more about Jim's voting strategy, for instance, if we knew where he lived, his previous voting habits, or if we simply asked him for whom he voted (in which case, we might also want to know how often Jim lies).

3.7.3 Induction by Shared Properties

Induction by shared properties involves noting the similarity between two things with respect to their properties, and inferring from this that they may share other properties.

A familiar example of this is how a company might recommend products to you based on other customers' purchases. Amazon.com tells me, for instance, that customers who bought the complete Sex and the City DVD series also bought Lipstick Jungle and Twilight.

Assuming that people buy things because they like them, we can rephrase this as:

(P1) There are a large number of people who, if they like Sex and the City and Twilight, will also like Lipstick Jungle.

I could also make the following observation:

(P2) I like Sex and the City and Twilight.

And then infer from there two premises that:

(C) I would also like Lipstick Jungle.

And I did. In general, induction by shared properties

assumes that if something has properties w, x, y, and z, and if something else has properties w, x, and y, then it's reasonable to assume that that something else also has property z. Note that in the above example all of the properties were actually preferences with regard to entertainment. The kinds of properties involved in the comparison can and will make an argument better or worse. Let's consider a worse induction.

(P1) Lisa is tall, has blonde hair, has blue eyes, and rocks out to Nirvana on weekends.

(P2) Gina is tall, has blonde hair, and has blue eyes.

(C) Therefore Gina probably rocks out to Nirvana on weekends.

In this case the properties don't seem to be related in the same way as in the first example. While the first three are physical characteristics, the last property instead indicates to us that Lisa is stuck in a 90's grunge phase. Gina, though she shares several properties with Lisa, might not share the same undying love for Kurt Cobain. Let's try a stronger argument.

(P1) Bob and Dick both wear plaid shirts all the time, wear large plastic-rimmed glasses, and listen to bands you've never heard of.

(P2) Bob drinks PBR.

(C) Dick probably also drinks PBR.

Here we can identify the qualities that Bob and Dick have in common as symptoms of hipsterism. The fact that Bob drinks PBR is another symptom of this affectation. Given that Dick is exhibiting most of the same symptoms, the idea that Dick would also drink PBR is a reasonable assumption to make.

Practical Uses

A procedure very much like Induction by Shared Properties is performed by nurses and doctors when they diagnose a patient's condition. Their thinking goes like this:

(P1) Patients who have elephantitus display an increased

heart rate, elevated blood pressure, a rash on their skin, and a strong desire to visit the elephant pen at the zoo.
(P2) The patient here in front of me has an increased heart rate, elevated blood pressure, and a strong desire to visit the elephant pen at the zoo.
(C) It is probable, therefore, that the patient here in front of me has elephantitus.

The more that a patient's symptoms match the 'textbook definition' of a given disease, then the more likely it is that the patient has that disease. Caregivers then treat the patient for the disease that they think the patient probably has. If the disease doesn't respond to the treatment, or the patient starts to present different symptoms, then they consider other conditions with similar symptoms that the patient is likely to have.

3.7.4 Induction by Shared Relations

Induction by shared relations is much like induction by shared properties, except insofar that what is shared are not properties, but relations. A simple example is the causal relation, from which we might make an inductive argument like this:

(P1) Percocet, Oxycontin and Morphine reduce pain, cause drowsiness, and may be habit forming.
(P2) Heroin also reduces pain and causes drowsiness.
(C) Heroin is probably also habit forming.

In this case the effects of reducing pain, drowsiness, and addiction are all assumed to be caused by the drugs listed. We can use an induction by shared relation to make the probable conclusion that if heroin, like the other drugs, reduces pain and causes drowsiness, it is probably also habit forming.

Another interesting example are the relations we have with other people. For instance, Facebook knows everything about you. But let's focus on the "friends with" relation. They compare who your friends are with the friends of your friends in order to determine who else you might actually know. The induction goes a little like this:

(P1) Donna is friends with Brandon, Kelly, Steve, and Brenda.
(P2) David is friends with Brandon, Kelly, and Steve.
(C) David probably also knows Brenda.

We could strengthen that argument if we knew that Brandon, Kelly, Steve, and Brenda were all friends with each other as well. We could also make an alternate conclusion based on the same argument above:

(C) David probably also knows Donna.

They do, after all, know at least three of the same people. They've probably run into each other at some point.

3.8 Scientific Method

The procedure that scientists use is also a standard form of argument. Part of it is inductive, and so like other inductions, its conclusions only give you the likelihood or the probability that something is true, and not the certainty that it's true. But when it is done correctly, the conclusions it reaches are very well grounded in experimental evidence. Another part of it is deductive; and like other deductions, it gives you certain knowledge - but it gives you certainty about what's false, not what's true! These two parts have to be put together in a particular way. Here's a rough outline of how the procedure works.

OBSERVATION: Something is observed in the world which invokes your curiosity.
THEORY: An idea is proposed which could explain why the thing which you observed happened, or why it is what it is. This is the part of the procedure where scientists can get quite creative and imaginative.
PREDICTION: A test is planned which could prove or disprove the theory. As part of the plan, the scientist will offer a proposition in this form: "If my theory is true, then the experiment will have [whatever] result."
EXPERIMENT: The test is performed, and the results are recorded.
5(A). SUCCESSFUL RESULT: If the prediction you

made at stage 3 came true, then the theory devised at step 2 is strengthened. This part of scientific method is inductive, and not deductive. And then we go back to step 3 to make more predictions and do more and more tests, to see if the theory can get stronger yet.

5(b). FAILED RESULT: If the prediction did not come true, then the theory is falsified. This part of scientific method is deductive: scientists can't always be certain about what's true but they can be absolutely certain about what's false. When our predictions fail, we go back to step 2 and devise a new theory to put to the test, and a new prediction to go with it.

Actually, a failed experimental result is really a kind of success, because falsification rules out the impossible. And that frees up the scientist to pursue other, more promising theories.

Scientists often test more than one theory at the same time, so that they can eventually arrive at the "last theory standing." In this way, scientists can use a form of disjunctive syllogism (see 3.6.6 above) to arrive at definitive conclusions about what theory is the best explanation for the observation. Here's how that part of the procedure works.

> (P1) Either Theory 1 is true, or Theory 2 is true, or Theory 3 is true, or Theory 4 is true. (And so on, for however many theories are being tested.)
> (P2) By experimental observation, Theories 1 and 2 and 3 were falsified.
> (C) Therefore, Theory 4 is true.

Or, at least, Theory 4 is strengthened to the point where it would be quite absurd to believe anything else. After all, there might be other theories that we haven't thought of, or tested yet. But until we think of them, and test them, we're going to go with the best theory we've got.

There's a bit more to scientific method than this. There are paradigms and paradigm shifts, epistemic values, experimental controls and variables, and the various ways that scientists negotiate with each other as they interpret experimental results. There are also a few differences between the experimental methods

used by physical scientists (such as chemists), and social scientists (such as anthropologists). But these things will be discussed in the expanded edition of this textbook.

Scientific method is the most powerful and successful form of knowing ever devised. Every advance in engineering, medicine, and technology has been made possible by people applying science to their problems. It is adventurous, curious, rigorously logical, and inspirational – it is even possible to be artistic about scientific discoveries. And the best part about science is that anyone can do it. Science can look difficult because there's a lot of jargon involved, and a lot of math. But even the most complicated quantum physics and the most far-reaching astronomy follows the same method, in principle, as that primary school project in which you played with magnets or built a model volcano.

3.9 Exercises for Chapter Three

1. Identify which of the following statements are propositions:

> (a) Tea time is at 2pm.
> (b) Why don't you love me anymore?
> (c) Please keep off the grass.
> (d) There's something wrong with kids today.
> (e) Thou shalt not kill.
> (f) Those 6 swans are looking at me funny.
> (g) Some people have trouble with propositions.
> (h) Can you pass the salt?
> (i) There's a hole in my bucket.
> (j) Could you be any more ridiculous?
> (k) 67% of statistics are made up on the spot.
> (l) Don't you dare kick that puppy.
> (m) Puppy kickers are evil.
> (n) This cat is my white whale.
> (o) My feet hurt.
> (p) There will be a sea battle tomorrow.
> (q) Parades are stupid.
> (r) You should probably not kidnap children.
> (s) Kidnapping is illegal.
> (t) Don't go into that barn.
> (u) Fa la la la la, la la la la.

2. Identify the following statements as a *simple statement*, *negation*, *conjunction*, *disjunction*, *conditional*, or *biconditional*.

(a) Lois is awesome.

(b) If you don't eat your meat, you can't have any pudding.

(c) You can go to the party if and only if your homework is done.

(d) You said you would give me a pony, but you didn't.

(e) Either you're going to the dentist, or I'll rip that tooth out myself.

(f) I'm a wussy little girl.

(g) "Hoser" is not an acceptable Scrabble word.

(h) Your professor is dreamy, and also so smart.

(i) If he kisses the puppy, he'll get the votes; and if he doesn't, he won't.

(j) Having a computer is necessary if you want to Skype with your grandmother.

(k) Happy faces are so 90's.

(l) Either you're going to eat this candy, or I will.

(m) I keyed your car, and I boil bunnies.

(n) You're not special.

(o) He didn't know what he was doing.

(p) If you hear sirens, you're supposed to pull over.

(q) You're going to work today, or you're not getting paid.

(r) I have a test tomorrow, and my paper is due.

3. Identify the form of the following deductive arguments. (Modus Ponens, Modus Tollens, Hypothetical Syllogism, Categorical Syllogism, Disjunctive Syllogism, Adjunction, Constructive Dilemma, or Destructive Dilemma)

(a) If you don't have a pencil, you can't write the exam. You don't have a pencil. So you can't write the exam.

(b) If you buy the farm, you can get kittens. If you buy a boat, you can go sailing. You're either going to buy the farm, or buy a boat. Therefore you can either have kittens or go sailing.

(c) If Lois has a bicycle, she also has a bicycle helmet. If Lois has a bicycle helmet, her hair will be flat. Therefore, if Lois has a bicycle, her hair will be flat.

(d) If you robbed that store, you would be found guilty. You were not found guilty. Therefore, you didn't rob that store.

(e) Kittens are either cute, or kittens are ugly. Kittens are not ugly. Therefore kittens are cute.

(f) I have two buttons missing. I have a tail. Therefore I have two buttons missing and I have a tail.

(g) All good muffins have chocolate chips. This is a good muffin. Therefore this muffin has chocolate chips.

4. Supply the conclusion that results from the following premises:

(a) P1: All monkeys like bananas.
P2: George is a monkey.

(b) P1: If this cupcake is less than a week old, George will eat it.
P2: George will not eat that cupcake.

(c) P1: Either you're lying to me, or I'm stupid.
P2: I'm not stupid.

(d) P1: If there's a monkey in the room, you can smell bananas.
P2: If there's a cake in the room, you can smell cake.
P3: There's either a monkey in the room, or some cake.

(e) P1: If you want to get ahead in life, you have to know your argument forms.
P2: You want to get ahead in life.

(f) P1: If you have a boat, people call you "Captain".
P2: If people call you "Captain", you get a lot of street cred.

5. Identify a problem with the following inductive arguments.

(a) P1: 79% of men who take drugs prefer cocaine.
P2: Princess Peach takes drugs.
C: Therefore Princess Peach prefers cocaine.

(b) P1: 60% of people who shop at Mountain Equipment Co-Op like mountain climbing.
C: Therefore 60% of people like mountain climbing.

(c) P1: 100% of the people I asked said their name was Joe Brown.

C: Therefore 100% of people are named Joe Brown.

6. Identify these arguments as either: *inductive generalization*, *statistical syllogism*, *induction by shared properties*, or *induction by shared relations*.

   (a) P1: Of the 10% of the population surveyed, most said they support the "kittens for all" movement.
        C: Therefore most people support the "kittens for all" movement.

   (b) P1: Kant's *Critique of Pure Reason* is a heavy book, densely worded, has a boring cover and if you read it in a coffee shop, people think you're cool.
        P2: Heidegger's *Being and Time* is a heavy book, densely worded, and has a boring cover.
        C: Reading Heidegger's *Being and Time* in a coffee shop will make people think you're cool.

   (c) P1: 67% of people who attend university never have the opportunity to commit armed robbery.
        P2: Bob went to university.
        C: Therefore, Bob has probably never committed an armed robbery.

Generalization Composition

Authority Popularity

Analogy Tradition

Novelty Herring

Appeal Force

Pity Fallacies False

Straw Man

Loaded Cause

Division Dilemma

Accident Ignorance

Naturalistic Amphiboly

Chapter Four: Fallacies

What is a fallacy? Simply put, a fallacy is an error in reasoning. A fallacy can arise for two reasons: (1) when we mistakenly assume that we have proven our conclusion when we have not, and (2) when we assume we have stronger evidence for the conclusion than we really do. Hence, when you commit a fallacy it typically means that you lack in some way the proper evidence necessary to support your conclusion. A fallacy does not mean that the conclusion is necessary false, just that the premises provided are not strong enough to show that the conclusion is in fact true. There are also fallacies that have faulty inferences at their base.

Why should we study fallacies? First and most importantly, so that you don't commit them. You want your reasoning to be sound and valid, and the surest way to meet these goals is to avoid fallacies at all costs. Second, learning about fallacies is a great way to correct biases in your own reasoning that are maybe too deep to spot on your own. You'd be amazed how much bad reasoning you learn from parents, family, and friends, your culture, or the city you've been raised in. This brings me to the third point, you want to learn fallacies so you can see the errors in reasoning others commit: Politicians, lawyers, newspaper reporters, bloggers, Wikipedia, etc. are just some of the list. Many times, fallacies don't just happen on accident; they are often committed with some kind of intent or reaction in mind. Spotting them enables you to make clear and educated choices about who and what to believe, to prevent falling prey to schemes or false opinions, and will enable you to communicate more effectively with others.

4.1 Appeal to Authority

(Latin: *argumentum ad verecundiam*) An attempt to prove a conclusion by an improper appealing to an authority, and this appeal is considered improper when the authority is irrelevant and/or unrecognized.

EXAMPLE: My mom says if I eat watermelon seeds, a plant will grow in my belly and I'll turn green. Because my mom said it, it is true.

It should be noted here that not all appeals to authority are faulty. When you are sick, you do visit your doctor and take their advice, and when you get into legal trouble you follow what a lawyer tells you. So, an appeal to authority can be relevant and proper when the authority you appeal to is: (1) recognized as having authoritative expertise in that area, and (2) if we ourselves lack the information, the experience, or cannot firsthand acquire the information required ourselves for the argument. To appeal to statements made by Buzz Aldrin when speaking about the moon's surface is a proper application of authority.

4.2 Appeal to Force

(Latin: *argumentum ad baculum*) Any attempt to make someone accept a proposition or argument by using some type of force or threat, possibly including the threat of violence. After all, threats do not establish truth whatsoever.

EXAMPLE: Company policy concerning customer feedback is "it's either perfect (100%) or we failed (99% or less)". Anyone who doesn't support this will be fired.

4.3 Appeal to Pity

(Latin: *argumentum ad misericordiam*) Any attempt to make someone accept a proposition or argument by arousing their emotions. A strong emotional appeal is meant to subvert someone's rational thinking. Remember: Pity alone does not establish truth.

EXAMPLE: The defendant should not be found guilty of this crime. Her life has been filled with endless abuse, a lack of love and respect, and so many hardships.

4.4 Appeal to Tradition

(Latin: *argumentum ad antiquitatem*) This fallacy happens when someone cites the historical preferences and practices of a culture or even a particular person, as evidence for a proposition or argument being correct. Traditions are often passed down from generation to generation, with the explanation for continuity being "this is the way it has been done before", which is of course not a valid reason. The age of something does not entail its truth or falsity.

EXAMPLE: We have turkey for Thanksgiving dinner and duck for Christmas dinner every year, because that is how my parents and grandparents did it.

4.5 Appeal to Novelty

(Latin: *argumentum ad novitatem*) This fallacy is the opposite of appeal to tradition, in that it is the attempt to claim that the newness or modernity of something is evidence of its truth and superiority. The novelty of the idea or proposition does not entail its truth or falsity.

EXAMPLE: String Theory is a new and rising research area in particle physics, and therefore it must be true.

4.6 Appeal to Ignorance

(Latin: *argumentum ad Ignorantiam*) The attempt to argue for or against a proposition or position because there is a lack of evidence against or for it: I argue X because there is no evidence showing not-X.

EXAMPLE: There is intelligent life on Neptune, for sure. Science has not found any evidence that there isn't life there.

4.7 Appeal to Popularity

(Latin: *argumentum ad numeram*) The attempt to use the popularity of a position or premise as evidence for its truthfulness. This is a fallacy because the popularity of something is irrelevant to its being true or false. It is one that sometimes is difficult to spot or prevent doing because common sense often dictates that if something is popular it must be true and/or valid.

EXAMPLE: Eating quinoa daily is a healthy thing everyone is doing, so it must be the right choice.

4.8 Accident Fallacy

(Latin: *a dicto simpliciter ad dictum secundum quid*) Also known as the fallacy of sweeping generalization. It is an attempt to apply a general rule to a situation with disregard for relevant exceptions to that rule. In other words, it is taking a general rule and attempting to apply it like a universal one (something that has no exceptions). Often what is being applied is what we would call 'rules of thumb', which are considered to be scientifically vague bits of reasoning that have a cultural and temporal context.

EXAMPLE: All birds can fly.

But there are flightless birds - like kiwi, penguin, emu, ostrich, and rhea.

If you were raised in a large city like Toronto, you may only see flight capable birds in the park or in your yard, and thus your rule of thumb would most likely be like that above – 'all birds fly'. So, what we are familiar with often determines the rule of thumb and what is 'normal'. We can discuss possible exceptions to the rule of thumb, where birds that are flight capable cannot fly, such as when the bird is a hatchling, or if it breaks a wing. One committing this fallacy would take instances like these and categorize them as 'abnormal' and still continue to argue that all 'normal' or 'quintessential' birds fly.

4.9 Amphiboly

A fallacy of ambiguity, where the ambiguity in question arises directly from the poor grammatical structure in a sentence. The fallacy occurs when a bad argument relies on the grammatical ambiguity to sound strong and logical.

Example: I'm going to return this car to the dealer I bought this car from. Their ad said "Used 1995 Ford Taurus with air conditioning, cruise, leather, new exhaust and chrome rims." But the chrome rims aren't new at all.

There are other kinds of amphiboly fallacies, like those of ambiguous pronoun reference: "I took some pictures of the dogs at the park playing, but they were not good." Does 'they' mean the dogs or the pictures "were not good"? And there is amphiboly when modifiers are misplaced, such as in a famous Groucho Marx joke: "One morning I shot an elephant in my pajamas. How he got into my pajamas I'll never know."

4.10 Fallacy of Composition

(Also known as exception fallacy) The fallacy of assuming that when a property applies to all members of a class, it must also apply to the class as a whole.

Example: Every player in the NHL is wealthy; therefore, the NHL must be a wealthy organization.

4.11 Fallacy of Division

(Also known as false division, or faulty division) The fallacy of assuming that when a property applies to the class as a whole, it must also apply to every member of that class as well.

Example: The US Republican Party platform states that abortion is wrong and should be illegal. Therefore, every republican must believe a woman doesn't have the right or freedom to choose.

4.12 Red Herring

(Latin: *Ignoratio elenchi*) This fallacy involves the raising of an irrelevant issue in the middle of an argument, derailing the original discussion, and causing the argument to contain two totally different and unrelated issues. A red herring has happened when you begin your argument about one thing and end up arguing about something else entirely different. This fallacy renders any premises used logically unrelated to the conclusion. A red herring is a distraction tactic, and is often used to avoid addressing criticism or attack by an opponent. This device is most commonly seen in political debates.

Example: The 'Occupy Wall Street' protesters complain that corporations and their money control Washington. But how can we take them seriously when their camps are messy, disorganized, with homeless people and drug addicts now living with them, and they are making life hell for the shop owners in their area?

4.13 Straw Man Fallacy

Like the red herring, a straw man tends to happen when one person is criticizing or attacking another's position or argument. It occurs when a person misrepresents or purposely distorts the position or argument of their opponent in order to weaken it, thus defeating it more easily. The name vividly depicts the action: imagine two fighters in a ring, one of them builds a man made of straw (like a scarecrow), beats it up horribly, and then declares victory. While doing this, his or her real opponent stands in the ring, completely untouched. The straw man is considered to be one of the commonest fallacies; in particular we see it in widely used in political, religious, and ethical debates.

Example: The Leader of the Opposition is against the purchase of new submarines and helicopters. Clearly he is okay with our country being defenseless and open to invasion by our enemies. He also obviously hates our country. So, be ready to learn a new language and give up all our freedoms!

4.14 Abusing The Man

(Latin: *argumentum ad hominem*) Any attempt to disprove a proposition or argument by launching a personal attack on the author of it. A person's character does not necessarily predict the truth or falsity of a proposition or argument.

EXAMPLE: All of Marx's economic doctrines are hogwash. But this was to be expected given he studied only philosophy in university, not business, and he never even held down a regular job.

4.15 False Cause

(Latin: *Post hoc ergo propter hoc*) This fallacy happens when one argues that because X happened immediately after Y, that Y was the cause of X. Or, when concerning event types: event type X happened immediately after event type Y, therefore event type Y caused event type X. In a sense, it is jumping to a conclusion based upon coincidence, rather than on sufficient testing, repeated occurrence, or evidence.

EXAMPLE: The sun always rises a few minutes after the rooster crows. So, the rooster crowing causes the sun to rise.

EXAMPLE: Once the government passed the new gun laws, gun violence dropped by 10%, therefore the new gun laws are working and caused the occurrence of gun violence to drop.

4.16 Non Sequitur Fallacy

(From Latin, means 'does not follow') A logical fallacy that is most often absurd, where the premises have no logical connection with or relevance to the conclusion.

EXAMPLE: The police have not been able to crack this homicide cold case, so they've called a psychic in to help out. They have tried all the traditional police investigation methods and the case still isn't solved. Therefore, the psychic (the non-traditional method) is needed.

4.17 Fallacy of the Undistributed Middle

(Also known as undistributed middle term) A formal fallacy that occurs in a categorical syllogism, when the middle term is undistributed is not distributed at least in one premise. According to the rules of categorical

syllogism, the middle term must be distributed at least once for it to be valid.

EXAMPLE OF THE FORM: All X's are Y's; All Z's are Y's; Therefore, All X's are Z's.

EXAMPLE IN WORDS: All ghosts are spooky; all zombies are spooky; therefore all ghosts are zombies.

4.18 Naturalistic Fallacy

(Latin: argumentum ad Naturam) A fallacy that occurs when a person bases their argument of position on the notion that what is natural is better or what 'ought to be'. In other words, the foundation for the argument or position is a value judgment; the fallacy happens when the argument shifts from a statement of fact to one of value. The word 'natural' is loaded with positive evaluation, like the word 'normal', so implied in the use of it is praise. One commonly sees this fallacy in moral arguments.

EXAMPLE: It is only natural to feel angry sometimes; therefore there is nothing wrong with feeling angry.

4.19 Loaded Question Fallacy

(Also known as complex question, fallacy of presupposition, trick question) The fallacy of asking a question that has a presupposition built in, which implies something (often questionable) but protects the person asking the question from accusations of false claims or even slander.

EXAMPLE: Have you stopped beating your wife yet?

This question is a real 'catch 22' since to answer 'yes' implies that you used to beat your wife but have now stopped, and to answer 'no' means you are still beating her. The question rests on the assumption that you beat your wife, and so either answer to it seems to endorse that idea.

4.20 Equivocation

(Also known as doublespeak) A fallacy that occurs when one uses an ambiguous term or phrase in more than one sense, thus rendering the argument misleading. The ambiguity in this fallacy is lexical and not grammatical, meaning the term or phrase that is ambiguous has two distinct meanings. One can often see equivocation in jokes.

EXAMPLE: If you don't pay your exorcist you can get repossessed.

EXAMPLE: A feather is light; whatever is light cannot be dark; therefore, a feather cannot be dark.

4.21 Begging the Question

(Latin: *Petitio Principii*) The fallacy of attempting to prove something by assuming the very thing you are trying to prove. In its form, the conclusion occurs as one of the premises, or concerning a chain of arguments the final conclusion is a premise in an earlier argument. This is a fallacy that rests on a circular argument.

EXAMPLE: All of the statements in Smith's book *Crab People Walk Among Us* are true. Why, he even says in the preface that his book only contains true statements and firsthand stories.

4.22 False Dilemma

(Also known as false dichotomy, black-and-white fallacy) A fallacy that happens when only two choices are offered in an argument or proposition, when in fact a greater number of possible choices exist between the two extremes. False dilemmas typically contain 'either, or' in their structure.

EXAMPLE: Either you help us kill the zombies, or you love them.

4.23 Hasty Generalization

(Also known as argument from small numbers, unrepresentative sample) This fallacy occurs in the realm of statistics. It happens when a conclusion or generalization is drawn about a population and it is based on a sample that is too small to properly represent it. The problem with a sample that is too small is that the variability in a population is not captured, so the conclusion is inaccurate.

EXAMPLE: My Grandfather drank a bottle of whiskey and smoked three cigars a day, and he lived to be 95 years old. Therefore, daily smoking and drinking cannot be that bad for you.

4.24 Weak Analogy

(Also known as faulty analogy, questionable analogy) When someone uses an analogy to prove or disprove an argument or position by using an analogy that is too dissimilar to be effective. Two important things to remember about analogies: No analogy is perfect, and even the most dissimilar objects can share some commonality or similarity. Analogies are neither true nor false, but come in degrees from identical or similar to extremely dissimilar or different.

EXAMPLE: Not believing in the monster under the bed because you have yet to see it is like not believing the Titanic sank because no one saw it hit the bottom.

77

4.25 Exercises for Chapter Four

Have a look at the following arguments. All of them contain a fallacy; some contain two or more fallacies. Which fallacy best describes each of them?

If you break the law then you should go to jail. Anyone committing adultery violates God's law. Therefore, anyone committing adultery should go to jail.

The sports section of the Globe and Mail is terrible. Those reporters don't know what they're talking about. The statistics are out of date and they don't even cover major events. That newspaper sucks!

The notion of global warming is ridiculous. In the last three or four years, winters have gotten colder and colder.

"If today you can take a thing like evolution and make it a crime to teach it in the public school, tomorrow you can make it a crime to teach it in the private schools, and the next year you can make it a crime to teach it to the hustings or in the church. At the next session you may ban books and the newspapers. Soon you may set Catholic against Protestant and Protestant against Protestant, and try to foist your own religion upon the minds of men. If you can do one you can do the other." (Clarence Darrow, The Scopes Trial (1925), Day 2.)

"Either you are with us, or you are with the terrorists." – U.S. President George W. Bush.

"The Jewish community worldwide is a powerful, wealthy, and influential group. So, all Jews must be powerful, wealthy, influential people."

"The animal rights people should not protest against the zoo. They should come out and see how much fun all the little kids are having. Everyone loves going to the zoo."

"It is immoral to eat meat, because raising animals to adulthood only to slaughter them for food is contrary to the ethical principles of a truly civilized society."

"Turmeric is a natural healer. In India, where the healing properties of turmeric have been long understood and accepted, you can buy Band aids saturated with the spice!"

[Senator Joe McCarthy] announced that he had penetrated 'Truman's iron curtain of secrecy' and that he proposed forthwith to present 81 cases… Cases of exactly what? 'I am only giving the Senate,' he said, 'cases in which it is clear there is a definite Communist connection…persons whom I consider to be Communists in the State Department.'… Of Case 40, he said, 'I do not have much information on this except the general statement of the agency…that there is nothing in the files to disprove his Communist connections.'

You can train a dog to fetch a stick; therefore, you can train a potato to dance.

On the basis of my observations, it is evident that wearing huge pants low on your waist, with your underwear showing, makes you fat.

I don't listen to country music. Therefore, country music is not very popular.

Some Canadians are animal rights activists. Some Canadians like to wear fur coats and leather boots. Therefore, Canadians are hypocrites.

He's not a criminal. He just does things that are against the law.

I'm a compulsive liar. That's why I can't trust anything that other people say.

This toaster costs $100. But that's a pretty good price, considering that a Ferrari costs $225,000.

"Everything comes to he who waits." Therefore, I'm not going to go looking for a job.

"Seeing that the eye and hand and foot and every one of our members has an obvious function, must we not believe that in like manner a human being has a function over and above these particular functions?" – Aristotle.

The "Occupy Wall Street" protesters are angry about economic injustice and the excessive power of corporations. But they are getting their message out using cellphones, cameras, computers, and the Internet – all of which are provided by corporations. Clearly, they're all hypocrites.

Geraldo says that students who cheat on exams should not automatically be expelled from school. But it's ridiculous to insist that students should never be punished for cheating.

My sweater is blue. Therefore, the atoms that make up my sweater are blue.

I'm right because I'm smarter than you. And I must be smarter than you because I'm right.

Your theory of gravity doesn't explain why the sky is blue. So it must be wrong.

My uncle Homer says that eating fish makes you smarter. That's good enough reason for me.

Sure, the experts all say that it's dangerous to ride a bicycle into the eye of a hurricane. But I have my own theory.

If today we allow voluntary, physician-assisted suicide, then tomorrow we will allow non-voluntary physician-assisted suicide for unconscious or mentally incapacitated patients. Then we'll have involuntary physician-assisted suicide on unwilling patients. Soon no hospital patient will be safe from these 'helpful' physicians!

Either we fire this guy, or else we send a message to all the other employees that it's okay to show up late for work. So we better fire him!

Bill is an investment banker, drives a Lexus, is over-weight, and votes conservative. John is also an investment banker, drives a Lexus, and is also overweight. John probably votes Conservative too.

Speaking as a professional chemist, alcohol is a solution.

The Mayor is a racist! At a City Council meeting last night, he said that he won't support our proposal to name a street after Nelson Mandela. How can we tolerate elected officials who say that minorities shouldn't have rights?

That is a lousy book. It didn't sell well at all.

I've never seen you get drunk. So you must be one of those Amish people.

In the city, you can always hear the sounds of car engines and aircraft, humming in the background. Therefore, you can always hear true silence in the countryside.

Reasonable

Chapter Five: Reasonable Doubt

Most people are familiar with the term 'reasonable doubt' from watching courtroom dramas on television or in film. It is an important legal concept which judges and juries use to help them decide whether an accused person is innocent or guilty. But reasonable doubt is something that can be applied to many kinds of situations. You might be asked to spend money on something. You might be invited to join a club, organization, or association of some kind. You might be asked to endorse a certain religious, political, or moral belief, for instance by signing a petition, or attending a rally, or voting, or making some kind of public statement. You might be asked to do something that you have never done before. In such situations, and others like them, it can be very useful to think of such requests as propositions, and then decide whether they are believable. There are lots of fairly straightforward ways to do this. And if you find that the argument is weak, or incomplete, or objectionable, or for any reason fishy, then it is probably wise to invoke your reasonable doubt.

5.1 What is reasonable doubt?

As we saw in the discussion of good thinking habits, reasonable doubt is related to healthy skepticism. We defined healthy skepticism as "a general unwillingness to accept that things are (always) as they appear to be". Reasonable Doubt is like a refinement or a specialization of the habit of healthy skepticism. Let's define it here as **the suspension of one's acceptance of some statement or proposition, due to an absence of sufficient support for that statement.** Here are some questions you can ask yourself, to decide whether some reasonable doubt is warranted:

- Is there decent and readily available evidence which proves that the proposition is true?
- Can you see that evidence for yourself?
- Can the proposition be put to some kind of test, especially a scientific test which could definitively prove that it is false?
- Does the argument in support of the proposition pass the test of Ockham's Razor? In other words, is it simple?
- Is the person who asserted the idea someone you have good reason to trust?
- Is it consistent with other propositions that you are already reasonably sure are true?
- Is it consistent with your world view?

The more of these questions you answer with 'no', then the more grounds you have for reasonable doubt. You can also ask critical questions about a few alternative propositions. For instance:

- Is there decent evidence that supports some other proposition, and/or which contradicts the one you are considering?
- Are there other, perhaps simpler ways to interpret the evidence that supports the proposition?
- What additional implications or conclusions can be drawn from the proposition, and are they:

1. Morally unacceptable, or

2. Inconsistent with the speaker's original intentions or world view, or

3. Inconsistent with some other part of the argument, or

4. Questionable for some other reason?

Again, if you can answer these questions with a 'yes', then you probably have good grounds for reasonable doubt.

A proposition is not automatically disproven just because someone could reasonably doubt it. You might have all the reasons listed above for why you should reject the proposition, and then later discover that it was true after all. But in such a situation, you have not made a logical mistake. The point of having reasonable doubt is that you should not be too quick to believe anything and everything. Rather, you should accept only those propositions which are supported by the best information and the strongest argument available to you at the time. If that information changes in the future, the good critical thinker also changes his or her beliefs accordingly. In general, Reasonable Doubt means **withholding one's acceptance of the unsupported statement until some acceptable source of support can be found.** So, having Reasonable Doubt is like having a "wait and see" attitude. It is open to the idea that the support for the statement may exist, but until that support appears, it assumes that the statement is false. Depending on your level of interest, you may choose to go looking for that support. But if there are decisions to be made or problems to be solved, and good grounds for reasonable doubt in your mind, then you will almost always be better off basing your decision, or the solution to your problem, on the best quality information that you already possess.

Here are a few examples of such situations where you should engage your reasonable doubt:

- A salesman offers you an amazing deal, but it seems 'too good to be true'.
- Your employer asks you to do something which falls outside your usual (or even contractual) range of responsibilities.
- An advertiser makes an improbable or bold claim about

the capabilities of a product that he's selling.

- A politician makes a bold claim about an opponent's character, history, or true intentions.
- Someone invents an unlikely new technology: super-fast computers, 'miracle' medicines or weight-loss pills, disease-immune genetically modified food, cold-fusion nuclear power, clean fossil fuels, perpetual motion machines, transparent aluminum, etc.
- A charity or a humanitarian aid organization asks you to donate to a worthy cause, but the critics say the organization might be a front for a private, for-profit corporation, or a missionary recruitment effort for a religious group.
- A film, video game, music album, or book suddenly becomes popular, and you want to decide whether it really is as good as it seems everyone around you says it is (and therefore, whether you should buy it too).
- A new friend tells you an unusual story about his family background, for instance that he is descended from royalty, or is secretly very rich, or was personally involved in an important historical event.
- You think you might have had a paranormal experience: seeing a ghost, or a UFO, or an angel, or the like; or someone you know might be describing such an experience.
- A health problem you might be experiencing feels like it might be worse than what your doctor tells you it is.

By the way: scientists have identified what they believe to be the area of the brain responsible for belief and doubt. It's the ventromedial prefrontal cortex. This area of the brain deteriorates in old age a little faster than other areas, which explains why elderly people tend to fall for scams a little more readily than younger people. Here are the summary remarks from the researchers who discovered this, as published in Frontiers in Neuroscience (an academic psychology journal).

"Belief is first, easy, inexorable with comprehension of any cognition, and substantiated by representations in the post-rolandic cortex. Disbelief is retroactive, difficult, vulnerable to disruption, and mediated by the vmPFC. This asymmetry in the process of belief and doubt suggests that false doctrines in the "marketplace of ideas" may not be as benign as is often assumed. Indeed, normal individuals are prone to misleading information, propaganda, fraud, and deception, especially in situations where their cognitive resources are depleted. In our theory, the more effortful process of disbelief (to items initially believed) is mediated by the vmPFC; which, in old age, tends to disproportionally lose structural integrity and associated functionality. Thus, we suggest that vulnerability to misleading information, outright deception, and fraud in older persons is the specific result of a deficit in the doubt process which is mediated by the vmPFC." [12]

And with that observation in mind, let's get underway.

5.2 Contradictory Claims

Suppose, for example, you log into your favourite Internet social network, and you get a 'friend' invitation from someone famous. Just pulling a name out of the blue, let's say it's from Matt Smith, the actor who currently stars in the BBC sci-fi television series 'Doctor Who'. The 'proposition' you are asked to believe, in this situation, is that the person asking to be added to your list really is the actor he says he is. But you probably have another proposition in your mind which states that famous people do not send requests like that to people they do not know. These two propositions cannot both be true at the same time. They contradict each other. So what you have to do is decide which one you have greater reason to believe, and which one you have greater reason to doubt. In this example, you have much greater reason to believe the second proposition. It's much more consistent with other things that are well known about celebrities. And you have some excellent alternative ways to explain who might really be trying to 'add' you: a friend of yours who wants to play a practical joke on you, for instance. Or it might be a salesman, or a con artist.

Contradictory claims are two (or more) propositions which cannot both (or all) be true at the same time. It might be the case that one of them is

true; it may also be the case that they are all false. But if the claims contradict, then it cannot be the case that they are all true at the same time. This is perhaps the easiest and most obvious situation in which you have good grounds for reasonable doubt. Here are a few more examples:

> "The stars in the night sky are actually pinpoints of light shining through little chinks in a cinder-block wall which surrounds our solar system."

You probably should not accept this claim because it conflicts with just about everything scientists around the world have discovered about the stars.

> "There are sharks and piranha fish living in the Ottawa river."

This claim conflicts with a few basic facts about sharks and piranha, and about geography, which are easy to find out.

Sometimes you might be given two statements that don't contradict any practical knowledge you have about the world, and that don't contradict your world view, but they do contradict each other. For example, consider these two statements:

> "Next summer, Heritage College will receive a multi-million dollar extension. When the work is done, our building will be twice as big!"

> "Next summer, the Heritage College building will be demolished and replaced with another, brand new, much bigger building."

Either one of these statements might be true, and they are both fairly consistent with other things that you might know about the building, such as that it is slightly over-crowded, etc. But they clearly cannot both be true at the same time. So, in this situation, you should doubt both of them, and then ask a few teachers or administrators what they might know about the situation.

Contradictory claims are one of the ways you can

83

---

12 Asp, Manzel, Koestner, Cole, Denburg, and Tranel. "A Neuropsychological Test of Belief and Doubt: Damage to Ventromedial Prefrontal Cortex Increases Credulity for Misleading Advertising" Frontiers in Neuroscience, 2012; 6:100. 9th July, 2012.

spot a scam or a confidence trick. We'll see more about such things later on.

5.3 Common Sense

How trustworthy is 'common sense'? Most of the time, it is about as trustworthy as anything you may have learned from your intellectual environment and your world view. But it is equally as open to criticism as anything else you might believe. For example: many people believe, on the basis of common sense, that shark attacks are common, that flying in an airplane is the most dangerous way to travel, and that having a shower will help you sober up more quickly after a night of heavy drinking. But all of these common sense beliefs are actually false. Only around ten people per year are attacked by sharks, out of the many millions of people who, at this moment, are swimming or boating in the world's oceans. Statistically, in terms of the number of deaths per year, it is much more dangerous to drive a car than to fly in a commercial aircraft. And when you shower after drinking, your liver processes the same amount of alcohol in your bloodstream as it would have done if you sat in your living room and watched television instead.

One of the reasons that common sense is not always reliable is because it changes all the time, and it can be very different from one community to another. For example, about a century or so in the past, common sense used to lead people to believe that animals don't feel pain, that Kings rule their countries by divine right, and that no one would ever walk on the moon. But today, common sense tells us that all three of those beliefs are false. So the next time that someone tells you that something is common sense, then ask yourself whether that thing is common, or whether it is really sensible. There's a good chance that it's neither.

Another reason you may need to occasionally doubt your common sense is because people often appeal to common sense to disguise the habits of self-interest and face saving. In this way, common sense is not a body of knowledge, but a kind of device for self-deception.

As a general rule, think of this: whether a proposi-

tion is true or false has nothing to do with whether it is part of your common sense. It might be true, or it might be false: but that will depend on whether it is supported by good reasons, arguments, and evidence, and not on whether it happens to be common, or seem sensical.

Of course, this is not the only way people use the phrase 'common sense'. Sometimes, people will refer to common sense when they are criticizing someone's choices, or holding them responsible for their actions. In this way, common sense means having a proper understanding of the likely consequences of one's actions and choices. And 'having no common sense' means having not enough foresight to predict the consequences of one's actions. This is a somewhat different use of the term. In that case, when someone tells you to "use your common sense", try to think of everything that applies to the situation that she is talking about, and what should be done about it. Making careful observations, and asking the right questions (skills discussed back in chapter one) are helpful here.

5.4 Emotions, Instincts, and Intuitions

Your emotions, gut feelings, and instincts should also be doubted once in a while. That is not the same as suppressing or denying them, of course. One's emotions can sometimes play a very useful role in the process of reasoning. And contemporary culture places a lot of emphasis and importance upon emotional knowledge. The lyrics of pop songs, and the dialogue in well-loved films and television shows, encourage us to "do what your heart tells you", and "if it makes you happy, it can't be bad." Pop psychologists, self-help books, and motivational speakers might also encourage you to "follow your bliss", "visualize success", and "believe in yourself". They might claim that we should always maintain a positive, optimistic attitude, and avoid excessive self-criticism or self-doubt, because they say such "negative energies" will attract bad fortune, sabotage our endeavours, and turn us into failures. But just like everything else, it is important to examine and evaluate what your heart tells you, just as you examine your common sense, and your world view, and anything that anyone else tells you.

Most emotions are triggered responses to some event, situation, or perception, happening either in the world or in your own mind and body. Sometimes the emotions are responding to things we may be only barely consciously aware of: subtle details, mnemonic associations, subliminal symbols, and the like. In this way, your instincts and emotions can be very helpful. They can warn of danger, or guide you toward beneficial ends, or (at the very least) inform you that there is more going on in the situation than is obvious at first glance. Many emotions are also triggered by our psychological desires and attachments, for instance the attachment to one's home, or workplace, or friends and loved ones, or future goals. We might experience irrational fear, anger, or even depression, when one of those attachments is threatened. And this can be an in-dicator of how deeply attached to such things you are. In this way, your instincts and emotions can provide you with useful knowledge, especially self-knowledge.

At other times, however, your emotions can get in the way of clear thinking. Stereotypes, prejudices, ob-sessive or criminal behaviour, and even self-destructive behaviour, are often supported by strong emotions. Someone who is excessively optimistic about his or her success in a business venture, for instance, might not fully understand the risks involved, or the true influence of factors beyond her control. Therefore he is more likely to make bad decisions. Someone who lives in fear of dangers that don't exist (someone afraid of being abducted by aliens, perhaps?) is not being benefitted by his emotions.

Furthermore, an emotional state is almost never a good enough reason, by itself, to explain or justify someone's actions. You might accept the explanation of a man who said that he ran from the burning house because he was afraid of dying there. But you would probably reject the explanation of a man who said he set fire to someone's house because doing so gave him pleasure. It can also happen that you are emotionally attached to something that you shouldn't be. Someone who, for instance, is absolutely convinced that he will get the job, or win the bicycle race, or get a very high mark on his essay, because he "just knows" that's what

will happen, and he is convinced of this for no other reason than because he "feels it in his heart", is almost certainly setting himself up for a colossal failure. And finally, it is possible to be mistaken about one's own feelings and mistaken about the right way to act upon them. A man who visits the home of a woman he loves two or three times a day, and who peers into her windows, and leaves notes under her door, and follows everything she does on her computer social networks, is not really loving her. Rather, it would be more accurate to say he is stalking her.

In cases where your emotions and instincts seem to be pulling you one way or another, or making you feel something and you are not at first sure why, then observe and question them just as you would any other aspect of your situation.

- Do you know exactly what you are feeling? Can you put a name on it?
- Can you identify what event, situation, attachment, or perception is stimulating the feeling?
- Is the feeling interfering with your ability to do something?
- Is the feeling interfering with your objectivity?
- Is a physical state in your own body contributing to the feeling? For instance, are you sleep deprived, or hungry, or ill, or have you had too much coffee lately?
- What are other people in the situation feeling?
- Are you feeling nothing at all? (This can be as much an indicator of things as an overwhelming emotion.)
- Has the feeling been invoked by something that some-one has said? And if so, can the statement be examined on its own merits, like any other argument?

Diagnostic questions like these can be hard to ask. Caught up in the moment, it might not occur to you to slow down, calm yourself, and observe and question your own feelings. But if you can cultivate the habit of casting reasonable doubt upon your own instincts and intuitions, you are more likely to make better, more intelligent decisions.

5.5 Looking at the evidence

Probably the most important occasion when you should exercise reasonable doubt is when you are told something is true, but there's no evidence that you can see which supports it. Or, there might be evidence which favours the statement, but that evidence is very slim and unreliable. Or perhaps the evidence can be interpreted differently, to support of much simpler conclusions. Here are some examples:

86

"Whenever American presidents visit Canada, their hidden purpose is to invite Canada to join the U.S.A. as its 51st state."

"The C.N. Tower in Toronto has a secret deck, just above the topmost viewing platform, which has special quantum-radio broadcast machines that control people's minds."

It is also reasonable to doubt a proposition when it's impossible for you to find out the evidence for yourself. The claim might be one which no one could verify. Or, there might be someone stopping you from verifying the claim for yourself. For example:

"I have invented a machine that uses cold fusion to produce cheap and abundant electrical power. It will fit under your kitchen counter - soon every household in the world will have one! But for proprietary reasons I will not allow outside investigators to open the box and see how it works."

In cases like these, a lot depends on how much you are willing to trust the speaker. In this example the speaker might not want to open the box because he is afraid that someone might steal his patent. A professional third-party investigator, such as an engineer or scientist, could be bound by a legal contract to not infringe his copyright. If you happen to know that the person is a competent entrepreneur with a graduate degree in nuclear physics, you might be willing to trust him, at least for a little while. But if you happen to know that he has a degree in theatre, not physics,

then you should probably keep walking. The overall point is that automatically believing what people you tell you should not be your usual and regular habit. And if someone asks you to believe something without showing you what's behind the curtain, you are almost always better off doubting it.

Suppose that there actually is decent evidence available that supports whatever it is you are asked to believe. Even then, there are several ways in which people 'skew' or 'bias' their handling or their interpretation of that evidence, to allow them to continue believing whatever they may want to believe, whether it is rational to believe it or not. The name for this kind of faulty reasoning is **confirmation bias**. The term was coined in Peter Watson, an English psychologist, in 1960, and refers to the way people tend to favour evidence which supports beliefs they already have, and tend to ignore evidence which doesn't support those beliefs. But when we downplay or ignore evidence that goes against our beliefs, we can end up making bad decisions. For instance, we might judge the riskiness of some action poorly. We might not fully understand new information which comes available. People put money into bad investments, vote for corrupt politicians, reinforce stereotypes, ignore health problems in their own bodies, and sometimes even reinforce feelings of depression and fear, because of the way they suppress evidence which goes against what they believe about themselves, other people, or their situation.

Three of the most common ways that people commit confirmation bias is by resisting contrary evidence, looking for confirming evidence, and preferring available evidence.

Resisting Contrary Evidence means avoiding, ignoring, re-interpreting, or downplaying evidence that goes against what you believe. Political activists, scientists, investors, religious believers, and people from all kinds of different professions will do this, when they feel their most cherished ideas are threatened. But if you want to test some statement to find out if it's true, you need to look at more than just the evidence that confirms it. You need to look for the evidence which refutes it as well, and in both cases you should assess how relevant or strong the evidence is.

Another part of confirmation bias is the habit of **preferring confirming evidence**. This means **favouring evidence that supports or agrees with whatever you already believe**. When we are particularly committed or attached to a certain idea, we often trick ourselves into seeking out and using only the confirming evidence. This can lead us to miss out on other kinds of evidence which are equally relevant. As a result, we can end up accepting a proposition that isn't true, or failing to properly understand a given problem. And we can harm our own interests in all the same ways that resisting contrary evidence can do. To cite a real-world example: in the years leading up to the banking collapse of September 2008, there were many people in the banking and investment industries who knew that a crisis was coming. Profits from debt refinancing, sales of derivatives, sub-prime mortgages, and the like, could not rise forever, they said. But those people were told to keep their objections quiet because the system, at the time, was still profitable. Some of these critics were threatened with being fired if they persisted with their warnings. But their warnings came true, with catastrophic results for the world economy.

Here's the example that philosophy professors almost always use: the proposition that "all swans are white". If you wanted to find out whether this proposition is true, you could look for white swans. However, even if you saw nothing but white swans, you would not be able to *deductively* claim that the proposition is true. At the most, you could claim that, "all the swans I've seen so far are white." Therefore, you should also look for black swans. The more white swans you see, the stronger your claim becomes. But one sighting of one black swan is all that it you need to *deductively* prove that the proposition is false.

Although it is not, strictly speaking, a part of confirmation bias, there is a third way that people inadvertently bias their handling of evidence: **Preferring Available Evidence**. This means **preferring the evidence that is easy to find**. The evidence might be memorable, or very impressive, or simply psychologically persuasive. It might be the evidence that happens to come up on your social media stream, as your friends share the website links or the 'memes' that

amuse or interest them. But the easy evidence is not necessarily all the evidence! For example: people today are inclined to assume that there is more war in the world now than ever before, because we hear about war in the news almost every day. But actually, there is much less war in the world now than ever before. In fact, at the time of writing, only 42 countries, out of 196, are considered war zones.[13]

As a final note about evidence: claims which assert something amazing, unlikely, or wild, or even just especially unusual, are often called **extraordinary claims**. So here's another 'proverb of reason' for you: **"extraordinary claims require extraordinary evidence".** And if that extraordinary evidence is lacking, it's best to assume the claim is false.

5.6 Conspiracy theories

A common kind of extraordinary claim is the conspiracy theory. For example, many people believe that the moon landings of 1969 to 1972 were filmed in a studio, the governments of the United States and other powerful countries are controlled by a secret society called The Illuminati, and that the attacks of "9/11" were an "inside job". Some of the inoculations given to newborn babies just after birth cause those babies to develop learning disabilities, and can even stunt their brain growth. Some people believe that the vapor trails in the sky left behind by jet aircraft contain mind-altering chemicals which governments use to pacify the populations in cities and keep them obedient to the laws. Extraordinary claims like these ones are often called conspiracy theories.

The American writer Mark Twain defined a conspiracy as "A secret agreement of a number of men for the pursuance of policies which they dare not admit in public." For our purposes, let's define a conspiracy theory as a **theory that attempts to explain some event or situation in the world by saying it is the work of a secret group of people who have nefarious aims.** Part of why conspiracy theories seem compelling is because there is often at least *some* evidence available which seems to support it. For instance, those who believe the moon landings didn't happen

13 Source: Global Security Organisation http://www.globalsecurity.org/military/world/war/index.html

often point to the photos from the lunar surface, in which there are no stars in the sky. Those who believe in 'secret government' type conspiracies point to the 'occult' symbol on the back of the American $1 bill (that's the pyramid with the eye in the top). And those who believe in various "9/11" conspiracies note that the World Trade Centre towers fell in a way that strongly resembles a controlled demolition.

But in most conspiracy theories, there are usually other, and far simpler, ways to explain the evidence. To continue the examples given above: There are no stars in the moon landing videos because their feeble light is drowned out by the glare of the moon's surface, dispersing the light of the sun. This is the same reason we do not see the stars on earth during the day: the glare of the sun, dispersed in the atmosphere, drowns them out. The "Illuminati Pyramid" on the back of the American $1 bill was placed there as a symbol that the American union is both glorious, and unfinished. It also has to do with the deistic and humanist ideas espoused by the authors of the U.S. constitution. And the World Trade Centre towers fell in an apparently controlled way because they were designed to do so in the event of a fire, just like all modern skyscrapers. Remember your Ockham's Razor! If other explanations are simpler, and require fewer presuppositions, then you should prefer those other explanations, until or unless extraordinary evidence appears.

Conspiracy theories tend to have these four assumptions in common:

5. They concern groups, large or small, not isolated individuals;
6. The group has illegal or sinister aims;
7. The group's activities are highly organized, not accidental; and
8. The planning for their activities is carried out in secret, not in public. [14]

If the explanation for some event involves these assumptions, and especially if these assumptions are closed to critical questioning (like a value program), then you've probably got a conspiracy theory. And you should invoke your reasonable doubt.

Some of you might have heard the phrase: "Just because you're paranoid, it doesn't mean they are not out to get you!" In the same way, just because some extraordinary claim bears these four signs of a conspiracy theory, it doesn't mean the claim is false. But it *does* mean you are almost certainly better off *assuming* the claim is false. In the spirit of open-mindedness, it's fine to remain open to the idea that some day you may indeed see some extraordinary evidence in support of the extraordinary claim. But until that day arrives, it's best to let the claim go.

5.7 Propaganda and Disinformation

Another place you are likely to encounter extraordinary claims which require extraordinary evidence is in political communications. In normal everyday language the word 'propaganda' tends to have a bad connotation: it refers to a message from a government or political party that tries to garner support for a political cause by emotionally manipulating people. But the word need not always mean something negative. **Propaganda is a type of communication from a political organization, which is spread for the purpose of raising support for that organization's causes and policies,** whatever those might be, and whether the means of persuasion is rational or emotional or something else. Governments publish propaganda all the time, as do all political parties, although some might do so more often than others. Corporations, labour unions, military forces, churches, charities, and all kinds of other public institutions publish propaganda to raise support for their own purposes, too. A political scientist with whom I'm acquainted defines propaganda as any government communication, or any party political communication of any kind, including innocuous messages such as those which inform the public about when a certain office might close for the holidays. But I think that definition is probably too broad.

You should examine propaganda claims with the same critical and skeptical eye that you use to examine advertising, or the news, or just about anything else in the mass media. Such claims might be true, or

14 Young & Nathanson, Sanctifying Misandry (McGill / Queens University Press, 2010)

false; but it's the evidence and the argument which determines that, not the source, nor the patriotic symbols which might surround it. But one should be especially vigilant of **disinformation**. Disinformation is a type of propaganda: it also attempts to raise support for a political party or cause. But disinformation tries to raise that support by **deliberately spreading falsehoods**. It might describe an event which didn't happen, or which happened differently than how it is described. It might accuse a person or group of doing something they did not do. It might warn of a threat from an enemy or a source of danger which does not exist, or which in reality is fairly trivial. It might discredit or divert attention away from well-evidenced facts or well-documented historical realities.

In some ways disinformation is not like ordinary lies, although it always includes lies. **Disinformation is also an attempt to construct a fictitious reality**, supported by a set of tightly inter-connected lies, half-truths, and pseudo-facts, and a carefully constructed world view. The purpose is not only to raise support for a political cause, or to influence people to vote, or spend money, or act in a certain way. It also aims to influence people to live, speak, and think as if the fictitious reality is the truth. Disinformation may point to actual events, but describe them in the very worst possible light. And it will normally appear to come from very trustworthy and reliable sources. These features help make it seem credible and persuasive. But this also makes it very hard to identify whether or not a given piece of propaganda is actually disinformation. And it is effective because most people tend to trust and believe what they see and hear and read in sources that look authoritative. And most people tend to trust speakers who seem confident, self-assured, and convinced. Here are some examples from the 20th century:

- U.S. senator Joseph McCarthy's 'communist conspiracy', 1950-54.
- The Nazi campaign against the Jews, which falsely accused them of doing things that are just too horrible to reprint here, 1933-1945.
- The corporate-funded denial of climate change and

global warming.
- The nonexistent Iraqi 'weapons of mass destruction', which was the stated causus belli for the Iraq War in 2003.

Almost all political parties and governments spread disinformation once in a while; some more than others, and some have done so in the past more than they do now. Corporations sometimes spread disinformation about the quality or safety of their products, or their competitor's products. They may also spread disinformation about the state of the economy, or the state of some situation in the world, in order to keep their investors confident, or maintain market share. Military forces sometimes use it to trick their enemies into believing the wrong thing about the strength of the force that faces them.

Disinformation is often extremely difficult to identify, at least at first. It often requires a lot of research, a lot of courageous questions, and a lot of time to pass, before the reality is revealed. As with recognizing conspiracy theories, one should remember that extraordinary claims require extraordinary evidence, but this, too, can be difficult to apply, because the disinformation may actually present the extraordinary evidence to the public. (The trouble is that such 'evidence' is often fabricated from nothing, or taken out-of-context, or mixed with half- truths and lies, or just as extraordinary as the claim it supposedly supports.) But there are a few general features of a disinformation campaign which, if you spot them, may give you reason to doubt it.

Excessive simplicity. The world view and the framing language of a disinformation campaign tends to presuppose a highly simplistic understanding of things. Elsewhere in this textbook I have described simplicity as a good thinking habit, and as a quality of the preferable explanation for things, and so this statement may seem incongruous. Yet the disinformation communique tends to simplify things that are by nature complicated, such as diplomatic, economic, or scientific matters. It also tends to ignore or suppress tricky or subtle details which nonetheless remain relevant.

89

ABSOLUTIST MORAL ASSUMPTIONS. As part of its excessively simple view of things, the disinformation campaign often assumes that in any moral matter related to its topic there are only 'good guys' and 'bad guys', and almost nothing in between. Within the world view of the fictitious reality created by the campaign there is normally no room for any discussion of alternatives. In this way the world view presupposed by a disinformation campaign resembles a value program (c.f. world views, chapter 1.)

FEAR. The 'bad guys' in the absolutist moral assumption are portrayed as a source of danger. They might be said to threaten the economy, or the state, or people's lives. Racist or xenophobic beliefs are frequently included here: the campaign might claim that the 'bad guys' cannot be trusted because they have lower standards of hygiene, or they are prone to criminality, less intelligent on average, involved in criminal conspiracies, or that they do not share the target audience's cultural and religious values.

UNSTATED ASSUMPTIONS. The disinformation campaign presents a set of pseudo-facts and then suggests implications or hints at possibilities, using framing words, rhetorical or leading questions, provocative images, and the like. The target audience is thus prompted to reach certain conclusions on their own. This technique is often used when the explicit statement of the assumption would damage the campaign, for instance if the conclusion to be reached is racist or sexist, or if it is clearly a logical fallacy.

TIME PRESSURE: if the disinformation includes a call to action, then it is often claimed that the action must be taken quickly. War propaganda often includes an element of time pressure.

MIXING TRUTHS AND FALSEHOODS. Disinformation campaigns might include a few clear truths among its propositions. Mixing truths together with half-truths and lies, and expressing such truths with the right kind of framing language, can help make the overall picture presented by the campaign appear more believable.

FAKE, INACCESSIBLE, OR MISQUOTED AUTHORITIES. Among the falsehoods which form part of the disinformation, there might be testimony from scientists, policy analysts, or other relevant experts and witnesses. Later, it may be revealed that these people cannot be reached by the public, or that their actual reports have been suppressed or partially censored, or that they don't exist at all. (One should always be suspicious of statements like "The experts agree that…" when such statements are not coupled with information about who those experts are, or what organization they work for.) Out-of-context quotations from actual experts, or from political rivals, may also be used to make it seem as if that person said something very different from what was actually intended.

SHIFTED ACCUSATIONS. The disinformation campaign might accuse rival persons or parties of doing things they themselves have done, including conducting disinformation campaigns.

BLACK PROPAGANDA / FALSE FLAGS. A disinformation communique might disguise its true source, for instance by appearing to have come from one party, when in fact it came from another. Or, it might describe a real event, with credible witnesses and documentary evidence, but which was secretly carried out by persons disguised as members of a different party than their own. The term 'false flag' comes from military and spycraft parlance, and refers to ships flying the flag of a different country than the one they're actually registered with, or soldiers wearing the uniforms of a different army than their own.

MARKETING TECHNIQUES. Disinformation often uses some of the same techniques used by advertisers to persuade us to spend our money in certain ways. It might use celebrity endorsements, weasel words, constant repetition, provocative images, and so on. If it comes from a government, it might use patriotic symbols such as national flags, portraits of respected leaders, references to historical events, and so on. If it comes from a religious group, it might use religious symbols, or quotations from holy books, etc.

90

There might be more to disinformation than these features, but these are perhaps the most important points. A given disinformation campaign might have only some of these features, not all of them. But the more of these features you think are present in a given piece of propaganda, then the more you may want to engage your reasonable doubt.

Another thing you can do is go to a fact-checking agency, to see if any professional research has been done on the topic. Most such agencies can be reached on the Internet, and some publish their findings in newspapers and magazines as well as in their own web sites. Here is a short list of them:

- FactCheck.org (USA)
- PolitiFact.com (USA)
- FullFact.org (United Kingdom)
- Snopes.com (primarily for memes and urban legends)

5.8 Doubting experts and professionals

Given that we don't always have the time or the opportunity to figure out things for ourselves, we have to rely on experts at least some of the time. This is natural and normal, and not a problem. But we must still decide when it is rational to trust an expert, and when it is rational to not trust one! And in some specialized fields, if you are not a professional in that field then you are probably not in a very good position to judge whether the expert has done a good job. It is also sometimes the case that professionals and experts are in a position to harm as well as to help their clients. So, how do you know who is an expert, and who is not? And how do we decide whether a given expert can be trusted?

One of the most frequently quoted definitions of a 'profession' was written in 1914 by United States Supreme Court judge Louis Brandeis, who wrote that a profession is:

> …an occupation for which the necessary preliminary training is intellectual in character, involving knowledge and to some extent learning, as distinguished from mere skill; which is pursued largely for others, and not merely for one's own self; and in which the financial return is not the accepted measure of success. [15]

We might criticize this definition by saying that its emphasis on service to others renders it too narrow. There might be lots of experts who practice their profession in order to benefit themselves. Yet the point that Brandeis was trying to reach was that such service to the public is an essential part of what makes a professional person trustworthy.

Let's define an expert here as someone who is very knowledgeable in a particular subject area or field, more so than most other people are, due to some combination of experience and specialized training. Experts tend to have:

- A lot of **formal education** and training from college or university, or some other reputable institution relevant to their field.
- A lot of **experience**. Several years at least; and the more, the better.
- A **decent reputation** among other experts in the same field, and among clients.
- A history of professional accomplishments.

Yet even when it is appropriate to call someone an expert, there are still circumstances in which it may be prudent to doubt what that person says. Here are some examples:

- The person is speaking about a topic outside of his or her actual training and experience, and yet claims to be an expert in that field.
- There are decent reasons to believe that the expert is inappropriately influenced or biased (for instance, by the corporation that funds his or her research), or involved in a conflict of interest.
- When various experts disagree with each other about the matter under consideration.

Regarding the second point: Many academic science journals now encourage their contributors to put a 'conflict of interest statement' in their published articles, to help allay concerns about whether corpo-

91

15 Louis Brandeis, <u>Business - a profession</u> (Boston, USA: Hale, Cushman, & Flint, 1933), pg. 2

rate or government power influenced their research. Here's an example of such a statement: "The authors declare that the research was conducted in the absence of any commercial or financial relationships that could be construed as a potential conflict of interest."

The third point deserves a closer look for a moment, too. Experts disagree with each other all the time, and this is part of the way that experts keep their skills sharp and their judgments sound. But most of the time, most experts in a given field will have a general consensus among each other about the most important principles of their field. (It would be weird, for instance, if there was a lot of disagreement among aeronautical engineers concerning whether propeller-driven aircraft need to have wings.) But when the experts have a lot of disagreement among each other, non-experts should stand back and exercise some reasonable doubt. When the experts who agree with some claim are the great majority, and when the experts who disagree with that claim are a very small minority, then we have less reason to doubt it. For example, the vast overwhelming majority of qualified scientists in relevant fields believe that climate change and global warming is real, and is being caused by human industrial activity. In late 2012 Dr. James Powell, executive director of the National Physical Science Consortium, surveyed 13,950 articles published in peer-reviewed, professional scientific journals. He found that only 24 of them claimed that the theory of global warming was false.[16] Clearly, then, there is no controversy among climate scientists about the causes of global warming.

And here are a few more points to consider. It is possible to doubt what an expert says without at the same time doubting that someone is an expert. It's also not rational to believe something just because an expert said it's true, and for no other reason. (To do so is called the fallacy of appeal to authority.) And there are some questions which, while we should seek the advice of experts for help resolving, we have to resolve for ourselves. Moral, social, religious, or political questions are among the kinds of questions each person should decide, by means of reason, on his or her own.

5.9 Doubting your own eyes and ears.

Most of the time, it's perfectly rational to believe that something is true when you've seen or heard it for yourself. Yet there are several factors that can alter your perceptions of things, and if those factors are in play, it can be reasonable to doubt your own senses.

Our expectations, stereotypes, and bad thinking habits affect what we see, and how we remember what we see. In 1947, psychologists Gordon Allport and Joseph Postman conducted an experiment in which they showed people a drawing of two men, one black and one white, confronting each other on a subway car. The white man held a knife in his hand. Later, the people were asked to describe the picture. Around half of them said the knife was in the black man's hand. Psychologists Boon & Davies replicated the experiment in 1987, and the picture they used depicted two white men, but one was wearing a business suit and the other was wearing workman's clothes. Again, many people recalled later that the knife was in the workman's hands. In these examples, the viewer's stereotypes and prejudices caused them to construct certain memories differently in their minds. Those who recalled the pictures wrongly genuinely believed that the picture was as they described it later. They were not deliberately telling lies. But because of their unconscious expectations, based on the stereotypes that still operated unconsciously in their minds, they got the picture wrong. This affects all kinds of situations where eyewitness testimony is important: criminal investigations, for instance. Because people's perceptions can be distorted in this way, police detectives prefer hard physical evidence over eyewitness testimony, when investigating crime scenes and bringing evidence to prosecutors. Eyewitnesses are often too unreliable.

Expectation, as a form of observer bias, tends to happen when we have a strong enough desire for something to be true. We will interpret our personal experiences in the way that best fits our desires. One of the most common ways in which we do this is when we see human faces in objects where no such shapes exist. Psychologists call this effect Pareidolia, which

16 Powell, James. The State of Climate Science: A Thorough Review of the Scientific Literature on Global Warming Science Progress, 15th November 2012

we can define as **a psychological phenomenom in which vague and ambiguous sensory information is perceived as meaningful.** And this happens because the mind is almost always working to organize the sensory information it receives, the better to understand it. The 'face on Mars', the hill in the Cydonia region of the planet Mars which looked like a human face in a 1976 photograph, is a well known example of this. Other examples of Pareidolia include astronomer Percivel Lowell's diagrams of "canals" on the surface of the planet Mars, first published 1895. The case of the piece of toast that had a burn mark resembling the face of Christ is another famous example. [17] The people involved in these examples strongly wanted to believe that what they were seeing is what they thought it was. And that strong desire affected their perceptions.

Sometimes, the mere verbal suggestion that things might be a certain way is enough to make people expect to see them that way. In 2007 I tried this out myself. On a visit to a cornfield maze with some children, near Halloween, I mentioned that the cornfield was the site of a War of 1812 battle, and that the ghosts of some of the soldiers had been seen there once or twice through the years. Sure enough, half an hour later, one of the children ran out of the maze, panting with fright, claiming to have seen one. He hadn't, of course. But the darkness, the creepy music fed through hidden speakers that the farmer had placed in the maze, and my suggestion of what he might have seen, was enough to produce in his consciousness the expectation of a certain experience, which he then imposed on his perceptions. Some 'Reality TV' shows exploit the psychological power of suggestion, to create in the minds of the show's participants the expectation of ghosts, or aliens, or whatever the show might be about.

Environments where the sensory information is vague or ambiguous can also influence our expectations, and affect what we think we see and hear. The situation might be too dark, too bright, too hazy, too foggy, or too noisy. Clouds, smoke, garbled voices, multiple sources of loud noise, blurry photos, strange smells, etc. might obstruct your senses. Because of pareidolia, the mind will often impose an organized pattern on the ambiguous sights and sounds. Similarly,

you may want to consider doubting your own eyes and ears when your senses are physically impaired. You might be sick, injured, stressed, tired, dizzy, excited, on drugs, hypnotized, distracted, disoriented, or drunk. Certain illnesses, such as diabetic myopia, can also affect one's eyesight. Each of these situations constitutes a kind of impairment, and can lead you to perceive things in the world improperly. It is usually under such circumstances that people have paranormal or supernatural experiences: ghost sightings, UFO sightings, etc. Leaving aside the possibility that such things are real: if you are seeing such a thing during bad visual conditions, and while impaired, it's probably safe to discount your first thoughts about what it is you are seeing.

5.10 Scams, Frauds, and Confidence Tricks

An associate of mine once saw a job listing on craigslist, in which the employer was looking for a mystery shopper (a person who poses as a normal customer at some business, and then reports about his or her experience back to the employer.) My associate was sent a cheque for $3,000 and then asked to wire-transfer the money to an address in a foreign country, and then report about her experience with the money transfer service. But when she brought the cheque to the bank, she was told that the cheque had the wrong signature, and would not be cashed. Had she deposited the cheque using an ATM, or a cheque-cashing service, then she would have transferred the money to the destination, and then the bank would have eventually discovered that the cheque was bogus and cancelled it. The result would have been that my friend would have lost $3,000 of her own money.

All scams and confidence tricks depend on two main factors for success: the victim's self-interest (especially his or her desire for money, sex, social prestige, a job, or even love and attention), and the victim's gullibility. They are successful when prospective victims want something desperately enough, and don't ask too many questions. Scam artists and con men tend to be creative, persuasive, and original; they constantly change or improve their strategies, so that their

93

---

17 "Woman 'blessed by the holy toast'", BBC News, 17 November 2004.

scams become harder to detect, and of course more successful. Some con artists will research their victim's history, and find out things like what the person wants, what their weaknesses are, what events in their past cause them shame or anger, and so on. These facts are then used to manipulate the victim later. Yet all cons depend on a fairly small number of basic strategies. Here are a few of them:

DECEPTION. Effective con artists use lies and half-truths to make themselves, or their situation, appear to be other than what it really is. Almost all confidence tricks rely on some amount of deception. They might dress in some kind of costume or disguise, for instance to appear very rich or very poor. They might pretend to be a professional in a field they actually know nothing about. They might set up a web site to make themselves look like a legitimate business.

DISTRACTION. Con artists keep your attention focused on something unrelated, while they or an accomplice steal from you when you're not looking. Think of the person who steals your purse or your wallet while pretending to accidentally trip and knock you down, and then help you to your feet again.

FLATTERY. Con men often open their game by being friendly and amiable, and quickly become admiring and deeply respecting. Some con men might pretend to fall in love with their intended victim. Since most people enjoy being praised and admired, this strategy helps make the victim more receptive and agreeable to the con man's claims and requests.

TIME PRESSURE. People who have been lead to believe that an important decision must be made in a very short amount of time tend to make bad decisions.

VULNERABILITY. The con artist might present himself as someone in pain or in a position of weakness, for instance as someone suffering a serious disease, or some-one persecuted unjustly by the law, etc. This technique manipulates the sense of empathy that most people have for the suffering of others.

OBEDIENCE. Most people still defer, at least partially, to lawyers, judges, police officers, professors, priests, rich people, and just about anyone who looks like they possess some kind of social authority or power. This is true even in societies that claim to be democratic and equal. Con men sometimes present themselves as persons with authority, in order exploit people's willingness to defer and to obey.

CONFORMITY. Taking advantage of the fact that most people will do what they see lots of other people doing, the con artist and accomplices will do something in order to make it easier for their victim to do it too. Think of people who start crossing a road before the lights have changed because two or three others have already started crossing ahead of them.

Although all cons involve those basic psychological strategies, some specific applications of those strategies have been so successful that they have been given names. Here are a few of them:

"BIG STORE" is named after the Marx Brothers movie, and it involves renting out a large building, such as a storefront or a warehouse, and filling it with furniture and people to make it appear like a well established business.

"PHISHING" is when the con artist sends an email that looks like it comes from a legitimate business, bank, or government agency. The message asks the victim to 'verify' or 'confirm' personal details that may have been lost or subject to a computer virus attack, such as email passwords and bank account numbers.

"SHELL GAME" and "THREE CARD MONTY" is a sleight-of-hand trick in which a pebble or other small object is placed under one of three cups or shells or similar objects. The position of the cups is then mixed up at random by sliding them across the table quickly, and then the victim is asked to bet some money on which cup has the pebble. What the victim does not normally see is that the pebble has been moved separately, and is hiding elsewhere, such as in the con artist's palm.

"Bait and Switch". This is a con in which a victim is offered a chance to buy something, or must do something to get something else in return. They might be shown the product or the reward that they have been offered. But once the money changes hands or the service is performed, the product or reward turns out to be something very different, and not what was promised.

"Honey Trap" is a very aggressive kind of scam in which a sexually attractive person lures the victim to a private location with an expressed or implied promise of sexual intimacy. Once the victim has been lured to the private place, he or she might be robbed, blackmailed, held captive, photographed in a compromising position, kidnapped, harmed in other ways, or even killed.

"Russian Bride" is a less aggressive version of the Honey Trap. In this type of scam, the con artists creates fake personal ads with dating websites or matchmaking services, poses as a single person in a distant country, and starts a long-distance relationship with the victim. Eventually, the con artist will ask for money to emigrate to the victim's country, and possibly to move household furniture and children too. But once the money is sent, the con artist disappears.

"Ponzi Schemes" are types of financial investment frauds. A con artist posing as a businessperson will offer to prospective victims a chance to invest in some low or medium risk enterprise, and offered an excellent return of investment rate. But in reality there is no enterprise. The con artist uses money from his second investor to pay his first investor. Then he uses money from his third investor to pay the second one, and so on. (In a variation of this scam called the Pyramid Scheme, the con artist freely admits that there is no enterprise to invest in, and promises to pay earlier investors with new money from subsequent investors.) This procedure can be very difficult for victims to spot, since at least some investors think they are getting their money's worth. A successful pyramid scheme operator can eventually become exceedingly rich, if he's careful. But the system depends on a constant flow of money from new victims to keep working. If the flow of new investment should slow

down or stop, the scheme collapses.

"Psychic Scams" involve a con artist who claims to possess magical powers. For instance, he might say he can communicate with the dead, or with angels or other supernatural beings, or with aliens, or even with God. For a price he will convey to the victim messages from a recently deceased person (or animal!). Or he might claim to be able to detect and remove curses. Or he might offer to cast magical spells which will bring the victim money, good heath, love, a better job, or some other kind of worldly benefit. Leaving aside the question of whether ghosts or magic or gods actually exist, the fraudulent medium exploits the victim's belief in the paranormal to part him from his money.

"Affinity Scams" are scams in which the con artist poses as a member of a tightly integrated small community of some kind, such as a church, or an ethnic enclave in a large city ("Chinatown", or "Little Italy", etc). The con artist ingratiates himself to the leaders and prominent members of the group in order to improve his credibility among other members.

"Advance Fee Fraud". In this type of scam, a person is asked to do something and is promised a large sum of money as the reward, but must pay the con artist a small sum in advance as part of the deal. A common version of this is called "Nigerian Money Scam" or "419 Scam", named for the section of Nigerian criminal law which covers fraud. In this type of scam, the con artist sends an email message to hundreds of people, in which he poses as someone from a foreign country, and asks for your help opening a bank account in your country. He'll say this is needed to transfer a very large sum of money as part of an inheritance, or tax-avoidance plan, or similar deal. You are also offered a share of that large sum of money. But once you open the account, you will be asked to make deposits to keep the account 'active' or 'viable' or something like that. And your share of the big sum never arrives. Another variation, going back to the 19th century, is called the "Spanish Prisoner". In this scam, a person asks for help transferring money to an individual who will help break a rich friend out of a jail (in Spain). The con artist asks for some money in advance in order to bribe the guards, and then promises a share of the money that the rich prisoner will surely pay as a reward when he is free. A more recent variation is the "Casting Agent" scam, in which the scam artist poses as a talent scout for a film studio or modeling agency. The con artist asks for large up-front fees for professional photo shoots, and promises the victim that well-paying jobs will soon follow. The photos for the victim's portfolio might arrive, or they might not. But the jobs never do.

96

5.11 Doubting the Mass Media

It is important to learn to analyze films, websites, video games, commercials and other visual media since they reflect and shape our cultural values. Critically analyzing media is different than analyzing an argument. The rhetoric of media is often about emotional rather than logical persuasion and this can make it difficult to determine the strength of the argument being presented. Our familiarity with different media and our viewing habits can affect how critical we can be. If you are used to watching films passively as entertainment, it is important to be aware of the things you ordinarily accept as part of the cinematic experience—such as the emotional quality of the score, or the use of close-up shots in certain scenes. These can have implicit premises that serve in both the arguments made by media and their rhetoric.

To begin analyzing media, you want to carefully describe what you are seeing. What is the media? Is it mostly words, pictures, sound or a combination of these? What is the subject of the piece, and how is it portrayed? Are the colors dark, is the focus sharp or blurry, is the lighting bright or dim?

Once you have a basic description, ask yourself what information the piece conveys and what you would need to know in order to understand it more fully. If it looks like an old film, you might want to know if it is old or if it is just shot to look that way. Think about how this would change the message. Does it matter who made the piece? Would the message seem different if it was created by a man rather than a woman, or by someone of a different cultural background?

Using this information, you can begin to interpret the media. What do you think it means? What message is the author trying to communicate? What other messages are also being communicated? Think about the emotional tone of the piece, and the attitude it takes to its subject. What values does it express or omit? If the piece presents itself as objective/ scientific/ journalistic what elements contribute to or detract from this? If it were personal and reflective instead would it be as compelling?

Media is meant to be communicative, so think about whom the intended audience was and what the purpose of the piece was with regards to this audience. It can be very interesting to compare commercials (for instance) for which you were and were not in the intended demographic group. What makes a commercial appeal to you, or not? What makes a film or game entertaining to you? How would a different audience respond? Evaluate the success of the piece in achieving its purpose. How did it intend to make you feel about the subject? How did it make you feel?

Finally, reflect on the cultural impact of the media and how it might influence others. Draw on all of your other observations to think about this. Does it portray the subject in a culturally acceptable way? Does it present it in a new light, or in a way that conflicts with other values? This can be very subtle. We often think that films made for entertainment, because they don't pretend to be objective or scientific, shouldn't be taken seriously. The film *Jaws* is about a man-eating shark and aims to scare viewers with tense music and sharp cuts. *Jaws* was a fictional film, but presenting sharks as predators to humans changed people's attitudes to sharks and had a negative impact on shark conservation. On the other hand, the BBC Blue Planet documentaries show the underwater world of fish and marine mammals as a purely foreign place without any human presence. While these films are beautiful, the way they present the marine environment hides the significant impact of humans on the oceans.

5.12 Doubting the News

There are literally thousands of sources of news and information available today: newspapers, radio stations, television stations, web sites, and publishing companies, large and small. It looks like it's a lot of different sources, but in fact most of them are owned and controlled by a relatively small number of corporations. Furthermore, not all of this information is of high quality, nor is all of this information of the same quality. There are several factors that can affect the quality of information in the mass media. By far, the most important of these factors is money. All news outlets, whether in print media, broadcast media, or online, and whether they lean left, right, or centre in terms of their political perspective, they all need money to maintain themselves.

News organizations make only around 20% of their income by selling products (newspapers, website subscriptions, etc.) Most of their money comes from advertising. Since that is the case, news organizations are usually very reluctant to report facts, events, opinions, or realities which might offend advertisers. They also tend to be very reluctant to report anything that might offend the shareholders, many of which are not individuals, but other corporations. And finally, they tend to be very reluctant to criticize political parties whose platforms are consistent with the interests of advertisers and shareholding corporations. Here are the words of Canadian news media owner Conrad Black:

> "If newspaper editors disagree with us, they should disagree with us when they're no longer in our employ. The buck stops with the ownership, [and] I am responsible for meeting the payroll. Therefore, I will ultimately determine what the papers say, and how they're going to be run." [18]

Here are some of the ways in which journalists, editors, and executives bias the news to avoid offending advertisers and shareholders:

SELECTION OF EVENTS TO REPORT / NOT REPORT: Obviously, if a news outlet chooses to say little or nothing about a certain event, it has biased its reporting of the facts, even if what little it does say is factually correct.

SELECTION OF POINT OF VIEW: As a general rule of thumb, any newsworthy public event can be examined from multiple points of view. Consider, as an example, a story about a bomb attack in a foreign country. The reporters could take the view of the victims and emphasize their suffering. Or they could take the view of the attackers, and emphasize whatever grievances they have for which they decided to retaliate. Or the reporters could draw attention to third parties harmed by, or benefitted by, ongoing violence in the region.

SELECTION OF FRAMING LANGUAGE: Nouns, metaphors and adjectives used by the journalists will often give away their point of view. War reporting is where this is most obvious: one side of a conflict might be referred to as 'troops' or 'hordes', while the other side might be referred to as 'soldiers', or 'brave women and men', or 'our boys'.

PREFERENCE FOR DRAMA: Most journalists know that their employers depend on advertising revenue for their economic survival, and they also know that advertisers pay more when the news service can deliver a larger audience. One of the most effective ways to draw an audience is to report stories involving conflict, tension, or controversy. Sometimes journalists will report two or more sides of a story even when one of those sides is relatively insignificant. This can make a controversy appear larger than it really is. For instance, very few people believe that the works of William Shakespeare were written by someone other than Shakespeare. But in the interest of 'balance' and 'fairness' a journalist might give equal time to someone who believes Shakespeare's plays were ghost-written by Francis Bacon. This creates the impression of a dramatic and vigorous debate, and that's what usually attracts audiences.

97

18 Conrad Black, quoted in James Winter, "Black's Plans" The Globe and Mail, 12 March 1994, page D7.

FALSE EMPHASIS, AND MARGINALIZATION: This is a term that dates back to the days when newspapers were laid out by hand, without computers. A story that the editors wanted to downplay might be given only a small amount of space on the page, near the margins (hence, 'marginalization'), or on the back pages. Similarly, an event that the editors want to draw special attention to could be given a more front and centre position, with tall block-capital letters.

PASSIVE REPORTING: This is what happens when journalists don't do their jobs. An agency that calls a press conference typically gives journalists a press kit along with access to people for interviews, and photo-ops for their cameras. Passive Reporting happens when the journalists simply copy the information from their press kits into their reports without doing any of their own writing, researching, or follow-up. Reporters do this for many reasons: sometimes they are just so busy that it's easier to just copy and paste the text from the press kit. But organizations who want their information presented in the best possible light sometimes manipulate the environment of the press conference to make the journalists more comfortable: offering alcoholic drinks, for instance, or free entertainment.

DISINFORMATION: It's an unfortunate reality, but some news organizations willingly publish disinformation on behalf of political parties, businesses, churches, or other organizations that they support, or whose world views they share.

Given these forces affecting the news, and these common ways that the news is slanted or distorted, how can an ordinary person become helpfully informed about issues that interest her? The main thing to do is to read about the event that interests you in several news sources, not just one. Among mainstream corporate news services, some will be politically right leaning, some left leaning, and some centrist; pick one service for each of these three positions and read all three of them. Also, look for independent news outlets, which rely on volunteer or 'citizen journalists' for their content, and which make most of their money from

volunteer donations or reader subscriptions. (With less of their revenue stream coming from advertisers, independent media tends not to have the same problem with advertiser-friendly bias that corporate media often has.) And if you have access to the Internet, you can read about world events in newspapers and broadcast media of different countries. Here's a list of news outlets that I read at least two or three times each week:

FROM CANADA:
CBC News (Centre-Left)
The Globe and Mail (Centre-Right)
The National Post (Right-leaning)

FROM THE UNITED KINGDOM:
BBC World News (Centre-Left)
The Guardian (Left-leaning)
The Times of London (Right-leaning)

ELSEWHERE IN THE WORLD:
France24 (France; centre-right)
Al Jazeera (Qatar; centre-left)
Der Spiegel (Germany; centre-left)
Deutsche Welle (Germany; centre)
The Economist (USA; right-leaning)
The Washington Post (USA: centre)
The Irish Times (Ireland; centre)
China Daily.com.cn (China; centre)

INDEPENDENT MEDIA:
ThinkProgress.org (USA; left-leaning)
Truth-Out.org (USA; left-leaning)
Rabble.ca (Canada; left-leaning)

A final note: Journalists are professionals, and all of them entered the profession because they think it is important for people to know what's going on in the world. (Well, that's what one would hope!) Most of the time, if any bias appears in their reporting, it is quite accidental, and certainly not a reason to distrust the profession as a whole. Nonetheless, in the mass media there is no such thing as 'a plain fact'. Information in the mass media is always subject to various forces

98

which affect how, when, and in what context, and in what light, it gets presented. Professional journalists know this. They do their best to be as objective and as impartial as possible. But we who read the news cannot simply passively accept whatever a favourite journalist or magazine might say. We have to read the media intelligently, and do our own thinking, in order to be fully informed when we need to make decisions like how to spend our money, or how to vote, or when to take a stand on a pressing public cause.

5.13 Doubting Advertisements and Marketing

All advertising serves just one purpose: to sell something. In general, all advertising tries to do this in one, or both, of these two ways:

- Making a favourable claim about the qualities of the product;
- Creating a favourable feeling in the mind of the viewer, for instance by being informative, or inspirational, or entertaining.

But all advertising, at its heart, delivers only one message: "Your life sucks, and my life is awesome, so buy my product or service, so your life can be awesome too!" Some ads may present this message in an informative or entertaining way. Some advertisements even have what deserves to be called artistic merit. But the job of advertising is not to help people make informed and rational choices about how to spend their money. It is to influence people to spend their money in very specific ways, on very specific products and services. Thus we are always justified in approaching claims made in advertising campaigns with reasonable doubt.

Here are some of the most common ways that advertisers do this:

IDENTIFICATION / ASSOCIATION: Using key words, images, sounds, or even provocative shapes, the product is presented in close association with something desirable. The most common object of association is sex: by filling the space with images of beautiful and sexually

available people, advertisers play upon our deepest and most human psychological instincts. (Realistically, however, you should remember that when you see a sexy person in a commercial, you have almost zero chance of ever meeting that person face to face, so there's no point paying extra attention.) But advertisers might also associate their products with good health, exotic locations, celebrities and their accomplishments, or a lifestyle of some kind (be it adventurous, or fun-filled, or wealthy, or simple, or otherwise enviable).

SLOGANS AND JINGLES: Catchy tunes, rhymes, clever puns and word play, and so on, can hold our attention for years. To this day, whenever I see certain brands of breakfast cereal in the grocery store, I hear in my mind the song that was played in TV ads for that cereal back in the 1980's.

MISLEADING / VAGUE COMPARISONS: Sometimes advertisers want to compare their products to other similar products that you might buy instead. But since they also want you to buy their products, they have to present the comparison in a slanted way. For instance, the text of an ad for a headache pain medicine might say, "Now 30% more effective!" Well, more effective than what? It doesn't say. Or, a car commercial might show two cars together with their prices, and boast that you will "Save $15,000 when you buy a MonsterCar!" But the price of the competition's car includes all the optional features like power windows and air bags, whereas the price of the MonsterCar doesn't include those features.

WEASEL WORDS: These are words which appear to make a definite claim about the product, but actually don't. For example, the marketing text for a lottery might say, "You might have just won ten million dollars!" Well, you might have, but the realistic likelihood of actually winning that prize is very small. A campaign for a department store holiday sale might say "Up to 60% off everything in the store!" But in fact only one product in the store is marked down that much, while everything else is marked down between 20 and 30 percent. Words like 'possibly', 'up to', 'as much as', 'many', and so on, serve as weasel words when they are just vague

99

enough to mislead and manipulate the viewer, without telling an outright lie.

PUFFERY / EXAGGERATED CLAIMS: Puffery is an exaggerated claim which is obviously untrue, but gets your attention anyway. I once saw a billboard advertisement for women's cosmetics that made the claim: "We make women so beautiful, other women will want to kill you." Taken at face value, this statement is clearly, painfully false. But the statement still creates the impression in the viewer's mind that women who use that product will become enviable. Similarly, television commercials for trucks or fast cars might tilt the camera, to make the vehicle look like it can easily drive up a very steep slope. The image tells no lies, but most people don't notice the camera tilt, especially if the shot lasts only half a second. So the impression left on the viewer is a somewhat misleading one.

PUSH POLLING: This is a type of advertising technique normally used by political campaigns. Large numbers of individuals are contacted directly, usually by telephone, and invited to participate in a survey. But the caller is not actually collecting data. Instead, the caller is trying to influence the contacted person's thinking about an issue (and her vote!) use a series of leading questions, rhetorical questions, and carefully designed framing languages. It might drop vague hints about the bad behaviour of a political opponent, or an innuendo about the unreliability or untrustworthiness of a party.

5.14 Exercises for Chapter Five

Consider the following situations, and decide whether it is reasonable to doubt what is claimed, and why (or why not).

Early yesterday morning, just as the sun was rising, Jeff spotted what looked like a giant sea serpent rising through the mists of the lake. Jeff has never lied before. He must have seen the Loch Ness monster.

Shelly has had a terrible month. She was in bed with the flu for a week, the pipes in her bathroom burst, and she broke up with her boyfriend. After all that bad luck, she is surely due for better times.

Two studies reported in the New England Journal of Medicine in July 2007 found that the risk of cancer, heart disease, and diabetes were reduced when the stomach size of obese patients was reduced.

I recently purchased a gold-plated, jewel-encrusted scale model of the starship Enterprise. But I keep it in a safety deposit box in a bank vault. It's so precious to me that I don't want anyone to see it.

These statues magically move by themselves, in the middle of the night. But only the very virtuous can see them do it.

Of course there was a cover-up! And the fact that you can't find out what really happened is evidence that the cover-up was very effective!

Everyone who "Shares" this picture on Facebook will receive a free Kindle Fire HD.

The MonsterCar Corporation is actually majority-owned by a conglomerate of foreign investors who use their profit to fund radical militant religious groups. So if you are driving a MonsterCar, you're supporting terrorism!

Every once in a while, you might notice the Internet access on your phone slowing down or stopping for no apparent reason. Sometimes it's ordinary net traffic. But sometimes it's the spyware on your phone, gathering all your phone calls, text messages, emails, web sites visited, and camera pictures, and sending them to the government. It even tells the government your movements, using the map software.

Right

"should"

Wrong

M

O

Unjust

Just

Good

"ought"

R

Evil

"must"

A

Virtuous

Wicked

L

"is right"

"is wrong"

Chapter Six: Moral Reasoning

In the discussion of Reasonable Doubt, we learned how to decide what to *believe*. In this discussion of moral reasoning, we will learn how to decide what to *do*. In this sense, moral reasoning is the most practical part of the process. When we reason about morality we build arguments, just like when we reason about anything else. But arguments involving moral propositions have to be constructed in a special way. This is partly to help us avoid the Naturalistic Fallacy. But it is also to help ensure that our arguments about morality are consistent.

6.1 Features of Moral Arguments

The main thing that makes an argument about morality distinct from other kinds of arguments is that **moral arguments are made of moral statements**, at least in part. A moral statement, as you might guess, is a statement about morality: **it is a statement that says something about what's right or wrong**, good or evil, just or unjust, virtuous and wicked. Moral statements are not like other propositions: they do not talk about what is the case or not the case. Rather, moral statements talk about what should be the case, or what should not be the case. Look for moral indicator words like 'should', 'ought', 'must', 'is right', 'is wrong', and the like. And look for the language of character-qualities, like 'temperance', 'prudence', 'friendship', 'coldness', 'generosity', 'miserliness', and so on. Sometimes, sentences written in the imperative voice (i.e. sentences which are commands) are moral statements in which some of the moral indicator words have been left out.

Thus, a sentence like "Share your toys!" could mean, "You should share your toys!" But to be fully logical, it's necessary to phrase imperative sentences that way in order to fit them into moral arguments, and find out whether they are sound. It's also easy to fall into the fallacy of equivocation. Words like 'good' can have a moral and a non-moral meaning: we don't use the word 'goodness' the same way when we speak of good snow boots, and good people.

With that in mind, which of the following are moral statements, and which are not?

- Peter should keep his promise to you.
- Peter did keep his promise to you.
- Human stem cell research is wrong.
- Some people think that human stem cell research is wrong.
- My mother is a good person.
- My mother tries to be a good person.
- This pasta dinner is really good.
- Finish your dinner!
- It's wrong to cheat on tests.
- Information gathered from terror suspects via torture can't be trusted.
- Torturing people suspected of terrorism is barbaric and criminal.
- You've always been a good friend to me.
- Proper etiquette demands that we treat guests with respect.

As mentioned, moral arguments are made of moral statements. This means that the conclusion is a moral statement, and at least one of the premises is also a moral statement. As we saw in the discussion of deductions, nothing can appear in the conclusion that was not present somehow in at least one of the premises. So, if you have a moral statement for a conclusion, you need a moral statement somewhere in the argument as well. Without one, the argument is an instance of the Naturalistic Fallacy, and it's unsound. Consider these examples:

(P1) It's wrong to steal candy from babies.
(P2) Little Sonny-Poo-Poo is a baby.
(C) Therefore, it's wrong to steal candy from Little Sonny-Poo-Poo.

In this example, P1 is a general claim about moral principles, and P2 is a factual statement. Together, they lead us to the conclusion, which passes a moral judgment about the particular case described in P2.

(P1) Jolts of electricity are very painful.
(P2) Some of the prisoners have been interrogated using electric jolts.
(C) It is wrong to torture people using electric jolts.

In this example, both P1 and P2 are both factual claims. But the conclusion is a moral statement. Since there's no moral statement among the premises, this argument is unsound. Now there might be an implied, unstated general moral principle which says that it's wrong to inflict pain on people. And some readers might unconsciously fill in that premise, and declare the argument sound that way. But remember, when examining an argument, the only things you can examine are what's actually in front of you.

6.2 Moral Theories

How do we know that it's wrong to steal candy from babies, and wrong to inflict pain on people? We know this because somewhere in our intellectual environments and our world views, we learned a few general moral principles. And there are lots and lots of moral theories that might form part of your world view.

Here's a kind of 'family tree' of the most successful theories of ethics which philosophers have developed over the centuries.

1: DEONTOLOGY, OR DUTY-ETHICS: These are theories which claim that there are actions and choices which are inherently, intrinsically wrong, no matter what the consequences are.
    1a. Divine Command
        1a.1 from scriptures ["theology"]
        1a.2 from personal experience ["mysticism"]
    1b. Natural Law theory
    1c. Kantian Deontology
    1d. Justice
        1d.1. The Just Society [Plato]
        1d.2. Distributive Justice [John Rawls, etc.]
        1d.3. Social Contract Theory [Hobbes, Rousseau, Smith]
    1e. Rights
        1e.1. Natural Rights
        1e.2. Human Rights
        1e.3. Civil Rights

2: CONSEQUENTIALISM: These theories claim that there's no such thing as an intrinsically, inherently wrong choice or action. The rightness or the wrongness of the act or the choice depends on the consequences.
    2a. Utilitarianism
        2a.1. Act Utilitarianism / Hedonistic [Bentham]
        2a.2. Rule Utilitarianism / Lexical [Mill]
        2a.3. Objective List
    2b. (Or not to be.) Ethical Egoism
        2b.1. Classical Libertarianism [Locke, Mill.]
        2b.2. American Libertarianism [Nozik, Rand]

3: VIRTUE THEORY: These theories state that the weight of moral concern is on the character and identity of the person who acts and chooses, as well as the habits he or she develops and discharges through her actions and their consequences.

　　3a. Mythological / Heroic

　　[Celtic, Norse, Greek, Germanic, etc.]

　　3b. Teleological [Aristotle]

　　3c. Religious [Aquinas, El-Farabi]

　　3d. Non-Teleological [Hume]

　　3e. Will to Power [Nietzsche]

　　3f. Modern Virtue

　　[MacIntyre, Hursthouse, Foot, Crisp, Slote]

By the way, I have drawn this family tree with three roots in the base, in accord with the observation by philosopher Jonathan Glover that ethics is founded in three main psychological traits which he called 'the moral resources'.

Different ethical theories base morality either on self-interest or else on one of the moral resources. They tend to urge the claims of one of these factors to be the basis of morality… Sympathy for others is at the heart of utilitarianism. Respect for other people, as a form of recognition of their moral standing, is the centre of Kantian ethics and of moralities based on rights. Concern with one's own moral identity is one source of ethics centred on virtue. [19]

In the next sections, we'll look at four major theories of ethics in detail.

6.2.1 Utilitarianism

MAIN AUTHORS: Jeremy Bentham (1748-1832), John Stewart Mill (1806-1873), Henry Sidgwick (1838-1900), Peter Singer (b. 1946), Derek Parfit (b. 1942)

STATEMENT OF THE THEORY: The morally right action is that which results in the best consequences. An action holds no intrinsic value; the value of an action depends solely on its consequences.

DISCUSSION: By far the most widespread and popular ethical theory today, Utilitarianism is very practical, and in most situations it offers a quick and straightforward solution to most ordinary moral problems. It has turned out to be very historically in-

fluential in the last 200 years or so, especially in major public concerns such as women's suffrage, the reform of prison conditions, the abolition of slavery, the welfare of animals and of children. Because of its emphasis on calculating benefits, harms, and preferences, it has also profoundly influenced modern economics and econometrics.

The core of the Utilitarian theory combines three main points. First, actions and choices should be judged only in virtue of their consequences. Nothing else matters. Right actions are, simply, the ones with the best consequences. Second, the only consequence that needs to be examined is the amount of utility that the action produces, for everyone affected by the action. Utility is usually interpreted as 'happiness' but can also mean 'pleasure', 'benefit', or 'well-being'. Its converse, disutility, usually means something like 'unhappiness', 'pain', or 'suffering'. The right actions are the ones that produce the greatest net result of utility over disutility. And third, when calculating the utility that is gained or lost as a result of one's choices, no one's utility is more important than anyone else's. Each person's entitlement to happiness is exactly the same. As Jeremy Bentham said, "Each to count for one and none to count for more than one."

Modern Utilitarianism was originally developed for use by legislators in the British Parliament. Bentham's idea was that law makers should ask themselves what consequences the policy or decision under consideration was likely to produce. He listed a number of ethical criteria with which to measure utility, including duration, intensity, number of people affected, and so on. Adding up all of these criteria in an almost mathematical way, he believed, would make it possible for legislators to come to morally correct decisions fairly quickly. When considering any moral dilemma, the right choice is the one that produces "the greatest benefit for the greatest number of people", or the greatest net benefit over pain for all those who are affected.

There are several different types of the theory. *Act Utilitarianism*, which was espoused by Bentham, measures the utility in the actual outcomes of one's choices. *Rule Utilitarianism*, generally attributed

105

to John Stuart Mill, holds that one should follow moral rules which have been shown by experience to produce the greatest benefit for the greatest number of people. This may look like a form of deontology, since it is a matter of obeying moral rules. But note that the rules gain their authority only from the consequences which tend to flow from following them. Thus, we have rules like "don't kill", "don't tell lies", etc., because we know that people who follow such rules tend to produce utility for themselves and others. Those who break such rules tend to produce disutility. If there is some situation in which following a rule will clearly produce disutility, then the rule should not be followed.

And the core concept of the theory, Utility, also comes in different types:

THE PLEASURE PRINCIPLE': As noted, Utility is normally defined in terms of pleasure and pain, happiness and suffering. And this can mean physical pleasure and pain, but the definition can also easily include emotional and intellectual pleasures and pains, such as love, or depression. And it can include social conditions that harm people such as political repression. In this type of utility, all pleasures are equal: thus the pleasure of playing a game of conkers can be about as good as the pleasures of reading Chaucer. Some pleasures might last longer, or be more intense, or affect more people, and so fare better in the calculus. But if all other factors are equal, so is the utility or disutility that could be gained.

SATISFACTION OF DESIRES: Utility is defined in terms of the fulfilment of people's interests, and people's getting of what they want and avoiding what they don't want. Sharing some features in common with economic theories about consumer behaviour, this understanding of utility probably has the greatest prestige and appeal.

LEXICALITY: an innovation of Mill's that was intended to meet objections to Bentham's Hedonistic theory, this concept asserts that some things are more worth desiring than others. The pleasures of Chaucer really can trump the pleasures of a game of conkers, since the latter (well, according to Mill) is a higher-order pleasure.

OBJECTIVE LIST: Utility is defined in terms of an objective list of 'goods' that, as experience has shown, tend to improve people's quality of life. There can be multiple lists for different cultures, societies, and times in history, which allows the theory some flexibility.

CRITICISMS OF THE THEORY: Probably the most obvious criticism of Utilitarianism is that its central principle, 'utility', can sometimes be ambiguous. Measuring happiness and pleasure, as some forms of Utilitarianism requires, is a bit like measuring a cloud with a ruler. Are sado-masochists experiencing happiness by inflicting pain on each other? The re-defining of Utility as 'satisfaction of preferences' helps address this criticism, but it has problems of its own. Some people do not know what their desires are; some find that once their wants have been satisfied they are still unhappy; some might have wild or impossible desires; and some might have a desire to hurt others.

Another criticism is that sometimes the actual consequences of one's actions are hard to identify precisely. Your choices might affect some people directly, others indirectly, and some only remotely. So which of them do you include in your utilitarian calculus, and which do you exclude? What about unintended or unforeseeable consequences? And depending on how you measure utility, an action can be conceived as having very different moral worth. Do you add up the average happiness of all people involved? In that case the net utility can be increased by getting rid of those who bring down the average for everyone else. (Think of political 'ethnic cleansings' here). Or do you maximise the total happiness? In that case utility could be maximised by some enormously large population of people all of whom experience very little utility individually.

A third criticism has to do with the way Utilitarianism might force certain consequences which are unjust. There can be situations in which the choice that produces greatest balance of happiness over unhappiness also results in a lot of harm or suffering for people who don't deserve it. Think of a magistrate forced to imprison or execute an innocent man in order to prevent a riot or a war, etc. In classical

106

Utilitarianism, it can be acceptable to do that which burdens or harms some, in order to benefit many others. As the character Spock from Star Trek once said, "The needs of the many outweigh the needs of the few, or the one." Committed Utilitarians regard this as a strength of the theory (and rightly so). But this can sometimes mean that an unjust act could be compensated for by other consequences which produce enough benefit to outweigh the harm. Those who believe in any of the more rule-oriented moral views, such as the Ten Commandments or similar religious moral teachings, cannot logically accept that claim. On the rule-oriented view, no amount of utility could compensate and outweigh the harm caused by punishing an innocent person, for instance.

6.2.2 Deontology

MAIN AUTHORS: Immanuel Kant (1724-1778), W.D. Ross (1877-1971)

STATEMENT OF THE THEORY: The right thing to do is that which is in accord with one's moral duty as determined by reason. The rightness of wrongness of the action is intrinsic to the action itself.

DISCUSSION: Duty-based or rule-based statements of ethics has been around for centuries, but the philosopher who did the most to lay out the logical structure of such statements was Immanuel Kant. As he saw it, the right thing to do has nothing to do with consequences and outcomes. It is the choice you make, the action in itself, which matters. And to be moral, the action has to be in accord with moral laws. So to figure out whether a choice you are about to make is in accord with moral law, he proposed a procedure called the Categorical Imperative: "Act on that maxim which you can at the same time will that it shall be a universal law." Basically, the idea is to ask, what if this course of action was a moral law for everyone? Would it still be possible to do it? If some course of action became self-defeating if everyone did it, then you shouldn't do it. For example, if you were considering telling a lie to someone, even an innocent and harmless one, then you should consider what would happen if everyone told lies, all the time. The result would be that no one

would ever trust anything anybody says, so when you tell your lie your listener would know perfectly well that it's a lie. And that defeats the purpose of telling the lie in the first place. As another example, you might think it convenient to throw fast-food wrappings out your car window. But if everyone did that all the time, there would be huge pile-ups of litter on roadsides everywhere, as well as traffic hazards from flying garbage, and a terrible smell. Civic authorities would have to bring in workers and equipment to constantly clean it up, thus making the disposal of food waste less convenient for everyone. So, it is wrong to do it. Kant's idea is that reason cannot consent to an action which, if it were a law for everyone, would make it impossible to do the action.

Kant formulated a second, more pragmatic version of his moral principle, called the **Practical Imperative**: "Act in such a way that you always treat humanity, whether in yourself or in another, as an end in itself, never as a means to an end." In this second formulation of the theory, Kant named an object of special concern, 'humanity', as a thing which deserves the utmost respect at all times. 'Humanity', here, means that which Kant thought made human beings special: our capacity for reason and free will. Kant thought that reason and freedom were intertwined with each other, and he thought they were so important that anything which exploits, reduces, interferes with, or subverts them is always wrong. He was not simply saying that one should complain or retaliate when someone tries to take your freedom away. Rather, it is a matter of respecting reason and freedom wherever you find it, 'whether in yourself or in another'. A choice is always morally wrong if it exploits someone's else's freedom, or uses another person as a means to an end, presumably a selfish end. For example, you might think that buying a pack of chips in a shop uses the shopkeeper as a means to an end, but the shopkeeper is (presumably) freely exchanging his merchandise for your money. So there's no moral problem. But exploiting the shopkeeper's generosity to get a pack of chips for nothing is using his freedom as a means to an end, and thus intrinsically wrong.

The 19th century Scottish philosopher William

David Ross produced a theory of '**prima facia duties**' (i.e. 'first glance' duties), which further clarify Deontological thinking and help make it practical. Ross identified seven such basic principles:

FIDELITY: to keep one's promises, speak the truth, be loyal to friends, etc.

REPARATION: to compensate others for any harms or burdens one might have caused them.

GRATITUDE: to show genuine thankfulness for benefits received from others.

NON-MALEFICENCE: to refrain from causing harm to others.

JUSTICE: to treat people equally; to treat others in accord with what they deserve, etc.

BENEFICENCE: to do good to others, to show respect and kindness to others, etc.

SELF-IMPROVEMENT: to seek education, to develop one's natural talents, etc.

Ross believed that in any given situation, one or more of these duties may apply. Some duties may carry more weight than others, and each person must evaluate this on their own, following something like Kant's imperatives. In cases where two or more of these duties conflict with each other, the weightiest of them should take precedence.

Kantian Deontology is probably the most influential rival to Utilitarianism. Almost all religious thinking in ethics is some variety of Deontology, for instance. Modern jurisprudence and legal thought still stems from Deontological principles. Moreover, almost all discussion of human rights is Deontological in character. The categorical rejection of slavery, racism, sexism, hate crimes, war crimes, cruel and unusual punishments, etc., and the protections of basic civil liberties like speech, association, privacy, *habeus corpus*, and freedom of conscience and religion, etc., stem

from Deontological thinking.

CRITICISMS OF THE THEORY: Probably the most widely mentioned criticism of deontology is that it might be wrong to always ignore the actual consequences of our choices. When we do things, our intentions do not always coincide with the results. One can do a lot of harm even when one means well. And there is always a possibility that doing the right thing can sometimes bring about harm to people who don't deserve it.

A second criticism has to do with conflicting moral laws. It is conceivable that situations may arise in which two or more of one's moral duties conflict with one another. Should you always tell the truth, even in a situation where doing so might lead you to break a promise, or fail to protect someone in danger?

And finally, Kant's Categorical Imperative is perfectly capable of supporting various trivial or silly rules, for instance "Always wear a clown hat when visiting the Queen."

6.2.3 Virtue Theory / Areteology

MAIN AUTHORS: Aristotle (384-332 BCE); 20th century: Rosalind Hursthouse, Phillipa Foot, Alistair MacIntyre.

STATEMENT OF THE THEORY: An action is right if it demonstrates the virtue that is appropriate for the situation.

DISCUSSION: Virtue theory is the oldest but also the trickiest of the theories. It tends not to ask if such-and-such an action is the intrinsically right one, or whether it will produce the best consequences. It asks, instead, what kind of life is most worthwhile, what does it mean to live well, and what must we do to flourish as human beings. The usual answer that a Virtue theorist supplies to these questions runs like this: to live a worthwhile life, we must develop certain virtues. So, what is a virtue? It is "a settled disposition of habit", as Aristotle defined it; it is a special quality of character, a behavioural or psychological disposition, even 'a way of being in the world'. Each virtue has a certain object of interest: for instance, courage is concerned with the management of fear, temperance with the management of pleasure, etc. Each virtue also has a certain role in one's pursuit of a worthwhile and meaningful life.

Now there might be disagreement among various theories of virtue about just what a worthwhile life actually is; and there might be some disagreement about what virtues are useful and necessary to achieve that worthwhile life. Indeed there are different lists of virtues, from different cultures and different times in history, such as:

THE HEROIC VIRTUES (from the mythology of early bronze age and iron age Europe): courage, friendship, generosity.

THE CLASSICAL VIRTUES (from the works of Plato and Aristotle): courage, prudence, temperance, justice.

THE SEVEN GRANDFATHERS (from aboriginal Anishnabe and Ojibway culture): Wisdom, Truth, Humility, Bravery, Honesty, Love, and Respect.

Although there are different lists like these, there is usually enough general agreement among those differing theories for their supporters to get along with each other. Some theories of virtue claim that the virtues are necessary for the attainment of ethical goals like 'leadership', or 'happiness'. Some emphasize that the virtues are closely tied to the maintenance of a certain kind of community, and the preservation of various personal and civic relationships. But all, or perhaps nearly all, theories of virtue hold that the having and the practicing of a virtue is self-rewarding: by acting and living in a certain way, the virtuous person gives to herself. Similarly, all, or nearly all, theories of virtue hold that a vice, the opposite of a virtue, is self-punishing; the vicious person gives to himself a stressful, difficult, and unhappy life. Thus, a quality like courage is clearly a virtue, because a person wishing to lead a worthwhile life would have to know how to face danger and how to swallow fear once in a while. And a quality like cowardice is clearly not a virtue, because the cowardly person is effectively controlled by his fear. Aristotle defined Virtue as "an excellence in the

service of a function or a purpose." There's a moral and a non-moral meaning implied here: a knife can be 'virtuous' if it is sharp, for instance, and that's not a moral statement. But Aristotle thought there was a purpose to being human: it is to use the 'faculties' or 'endowments of nature' which he thought are unique to us, and not shared with other animals. Using those talents and skills, and developing them to excellence, is what makes us happiest in life. The most important of these talents, he says, is our power of reason. The important task which reason plays among the virtues is to show how much of a virtue is too much, and how much is not enough. This principle is now called **The Doctrine of the Mean**. A vice, Aristotle would say, is manifesting too much or too little of the particular quality that a situation calls for. Courage, to continue the example, goes between rashness or recklessness (which is too much courage), and cowardice (which is too little.) The idea is often compared to archery: your arrow can fly too high or too low, and in either case miss the target.

And finally, most theories of virtue emphasize that developing virtue takes time. Just as "one swallow does not make a spring", as Aristotle said, one good action by itself does not make one virtuous. Virtue theory requires one to practice a certain form of behaviour over the spread of one's life. One becomes courageous by making courageous choices and doing courageous things. Eventually, habit takes over and then you don't need to be quite as calculating about your choices. But even so, the virtues must be deliberately chosen, in each moment that calls upon you for a moral response.

CRITICISMS OF THE THEORY: One of the obvious problems with virtue is that the theory may not appear well suited to solving practical problems. When faced with a specific practical question such as is likely to arise in a business environment, or a hospital, or an arts venue, for instance, virtue theory tends to return rather unhelpful answers. It isn't impossible to apply virtue theory to practical ethics problems, but neither is it easy. (Imagine a conversation like this one. A client says, "We are having a fiscal imbalance. Should I fix this problem by cutting worker's wages or laying some of them off?" The philosopher replies, "Only if doing so

109

would be virtuous…")

Some critics have pointed to deficiencies in the definition of a virtue itself. Aristotle's definition of a virtue as 'a settled disposition of habit' might not be a good enough explanation of what a virtue is. Every moral theory faces a criticism like this one, that is, a question about the meaning of its core concepts. But as it faces virtue theory, the problem lies in the conundrum of 'deliberately choosing' that which we have a 'settled disposition of habit' to do.

110   ## 6.2.4 (Distributive) Justice

MAIN AUTHOR: John Rawls (1921-2002)

STATEMENT OF THE THEORY: The just distribution of social goods is a distribution that is advantageous to everyone. An unequal distribution can be just if it increases the total wealth, and also maximises the size of the minimum share.

DISCUSSION: Unlike the three theories of ethics discussed above, Justice is not a theory about individual choices. It is a theory of social and sometimes political choices.

There are, of course, many theories of justice, but the one I will focus un here is perhaps the most widely discussed and accepted: the theory by American philosopher John Rawls. Since his flagship text "A Theory of Justice" was published in 1971, literally all discussion of justice among philosophers has somehow revolved around his ideas: promoting them, modifying them, criticizing and rejecting them, but nonetheless talking about them.

Whatever else justice may be, and whoever's theory of justice we are talking about, justice is a principle of social organisation, concerning the distribution of social goods such as wealth, power, material resources, punishments and honours, and the like. The first line of Rawls famous theory confirms the ancient orientation of justice toward the public realm: "Justice is the first virtue of social institutions, as truth is of systems of thought". So when we speak of 'distributive' justice, we're speaking of the fairness of how we distribute those social goods. Rawls claimed that social goods must be distributed in a way that is advantageous to everyone. Note that he does not say they have to be distributed equally. There could be advantages for everyone gained by an unequal distribution. This leads to what Rawls calls **The Difference Principle**: any inequalities in the distribution must be acceptable to those who receive the smallest share. In his words: "The social order is not to establish and secure the more attractive prospects of those better off unless doing so is to the advantage of those less fortunate." Thus, Rawls claims that some forms of inequalities may still be just: they are just if they are to the benefit of the least well off. Under such a principle, injustice is not simply inequality, but rather injustice inequalities that are not to the benefit of everyone, and especially injustices which are not to the benefit of the least well-off person.

This is, he says, the system of distribution which all rational parties would choose if they were in an "original position", standing "behind a veil of ignorance". That is to say, it is the system of just distribution everyone would choose if no one knew what his or her social position would be, nor what share he or she would receive. In the "original position", one can know the basic structure of society but one can not know whether one will end up rich or poor, male or female, black or white, well educated or poorly educated, and so on. Rawls claims that someone in such a position would bet that they might end up as the person with the smallest share, and would therefore want that smallest share to be as large as it can be.

CRITICISMS OF THE THEORY: Rawls presupposes that in the "original position", people are still self-interested, and they want to maximize the size of their own share; and this Rawls identifies as rational behaviour. Some of Rawls' critics have questioned this assumption about rationality. There may be other models of rationality that do not presuppose self-maximization: for instance it may be rational to be charitable, sympathetic, and caring.

Some critics have also pointed out that not everyone gets to sit at the bargaining table where the social goods get distributed. Children, people with certain kinds of disabilities, people from foreign societies, even animals and the environment, have a stake in the shape of the distribution arrangement. But they might not be able to speak on their own behalf, and so their interests in how the social goods get divided up may go unrepresented, and they may thus end up unjustly deprived of a fair share.

Finally, Rawls' toughest critics have noted that Rawls' theory concerns the distribution of goods, and says nothing about what is owed to people, and nothing about what qualities or attributes a person might possess which entitles him or her to a share of the society's goods. Therefore, it may be argued, Rawls' theory is not a theory of justice at all, but rather a disguised form of Utilitarianism.

6.3 Summary remarks: Why can't we all just get along?

Why is there so much violence, conflict, fear, and hate in the world? Why can't people just get over it and be friends? These are, of course, among of the oldest and most difficult of moral questions. There are hundreds of answers, and none of those answers were easily discovered. It might be that there are just not enough of the good things in life for everyone to have as much as they want. So as people discover this they end up distrusting each other, and they compete with each other to get as much of those things as they can. Or so Thomas Hobbes argued. It might be that most people cannot stand the presence of others whose thinking and reasoning is radically different from their own, as David Hume once claimed. Perhaps it is as Plato said, that as people grow accustomed to pleasures and luxury goods, so they eventually become unable to restrain their appetites for those things. Therefore, like "a city with a fever", they turn to their neighbours, to take by stealth, or even steal by force, what they think they need to satisfy their feverish demands. Or, it might be that some people are just naturally, inexplicably evil. "Some men just want to watch the world burn," as Alfred said to Bruce Wayne in The Dark Knight (2008), although that answer always seemed to me too superficial, too quick, and too easy. People have reasons for doing things - reasons that are irrational, faulty, silly, or perhaps demonstrably insane – but they have their reasons, nonetheless. In the ten worst public shooting

incidents in the United States, 170 people were killed, not including the shooters themselves (five of whom took their own lives).[20] The shooter's reasons ranged from the calculated, such as the desire to terrorize people who held differing political beliefs, to the absurd, such as the desire to be seen on the media.

Let's re-phrase the question a little bit. What must people do to have *at least a chance*, even if only a small one, to get along with each other? That I think I can answer: *we have to talk to each other*. We have to be willing to speak truly and listen attentively to each other. There is a logical disjunction between speaking and hating; there's a gulf as wide as the ocean between dialogue and murder. You might want to 'send a message' to someone (as the euphemism goes) by beating him up, or depriving him of his rights or his dignity, or even by killing him. But the recipient of that kind of message is never in a position to hear it: the very means of delivery itself logically excludes meaningful communication. Think of old Lucretius here, who taught us to have no fear of death because "While one lives one does not die; when one dies there is no one there for death to claim; thus death never reaches you." In the same way, a message whose means of delivery kills the recipient finds no one at the point of delivery able to receive the message at all. It's very similar for a message delivered by shouting, threatening, bullying, stealing, hating, or any other oppressive or dehumanizing act short of killing. The message whose means of delivery oppresses or dehumanizes the recipient quickly finds that the recipient's ability to hear the message is stripped away.

But if we talk to each other, without threats, without violence, and without oppression, we acknowledge each other's humanity. This is because to speak to someone is to assume that the other person can hear and understand what you are saying, and to assume that the other person is capable of responding to you. The ability to understand and to respond, so it seems to me, is an important part of what it is to be human. Even to criticize and to disagree with someone is still to treat that person as a human being with a mind of her own, because criticism and disagreement hopes to persuade the other person to change her mind. (Thus

111

to criticize and disagree with someone is not the same as to take away that person's right to speak. But I digress.) Similarly, to listen to someone is to assume that the other person has a mind of her own, and that she has something to say, and deserves a hearing. Listening is not just the opposite of silencing, marginalizing, ignoring, or fighting the other person; listening is also a way of showing respect. While we are speaking to each other, we might also be confronting, competing, distrusting, manipulating, dominating, or even lying to each other. But we are not killing each other. And that, it seems to me, is no small thing. It introduces a moral dimension into the very structure of logic itself. While we are manipulating, dominating, or lying to each other, and so on, that moral dimension remains tiny and fragile, almost too small to notice. But it is not nothing. And it can grow. It appears on a scale of intensity: the less fear and hate there is in our dialogue with each other, the more humanity there is.

There may be reasons to reject this rosy picture I've painted. Jean-Jacques Rousseau observed, correctly I think, that rationality has power enough to separate people as much as to unite them, and that one can use reason to care less about people rather than to care more.

> It is reason which turns man's mind back upon itself, and divides him from everything that could disturb or afflict him. It is philosophy that isolates him, and bids him say, at the sight of the misfortune of others, 'Perish if you will; I am secure'… A murder may with impunity be committed under his window; he has only to put his hands to his ears and argue a little with himself, to prevent nature, which is shocked within him, from identifying itself with the unfortunate sufferer. [21]

But surely the problem here is not in rationality itself, but in a kind of reductionism that identifies reason with self-interest. For rationality is more than that. Reason can, indeed, find ways to reject the moral claims of others and secure itself in its own world, as Rousseau claims. But reason can also show us the moral worth of our neighbours, and create new ways for people to be friends. Rousseau correctly grasps the

former but not the latter, and thus his understanding is too narrow. Moreover, Rousseau portrays reasoning as an activity that takes place entirely within one's own mind, and nowhere else; but this is not always true. Reasoning, especially in matters of ethics, is also a social event. It enters into dialogue with others; it speaks to people and it hears what they have to say; and it tests its arguments against the criticisms of others. And if talking to each other does not guarantee that we will get along with each other, at least it opens the possibility. And that is something that violence and the threat of violence cannot do.

This textbook was written during the volunteer hours of its contributors, and financially supported by volunteering donors. I hope that all of them believe, as I do, that a world in which people can think and speak rationally is a better world. I've made this textbook available to the world for free, in the hope that it will help people understand each other, solve their problems, and get along with each other.

6.4 Exercises for Moral Reasoning

Examine the argument in the summary remarks given above. What are the moral propositions? What are the factual propositions? What patterns of argumentation (from chapter 3) are used here? Does the author commit any major logical fallacies (from chapter 4)? Which of the four main theories of ethics does it appear to presuppose? What does this essay say about the author's world view? And finally, is the argument sound or unsound? (Notice that even if you decide that it is unsound, we will be speaking to each other, and not killing each other…)

21 Rousseau, Discourse on the Origin of Inequality, trans. G.D.H. Cole (Everyman's Library)

Index

116

Made in the USA
Middletown, DE
10 January 2018